SHEREBAR. BETRAYAL OF THE INNOCENT.

BOOK 2

M M JUNIPER

lemon meringue
PUBLISHING

Cover art: D- Keine
Cover design by Lizzie Chantree

Created with Vellum

Betrayal of the Innocent

Sherebar book 2

ABOUT THIS EDITION

Betrayal of the Innocent is written and edited in British English rather than American English. This includes spelling, grammar, and punctuation.

With a big thank you to Lizzie Chantree for the cover design, advice, and support, and to Nicky Edwards for your patience and editing.

CHARACTER LIST

Sherebar the next chapter. Betrayal of the Innocent

List of main Characters from Sherebar. Book 1

Sherebar

A man who has lived through the ages, to be able to help the world in a disaster that had been foretold in the future. He has lost many he loved in his long life, but his genes may help some, now living, to survive.

Derebar

The spirit of Sherebar's twin brother, who had died at birth and was determined to destroy his brother and those Sherebar loved.

Jenny

A designer and programmer who has dreamt of Sherebar since a child. He told her about his life in her vivid dreams. In love with Doug, a doctor she met when writing programmes for his doctors' practice.

Val

A homeopathic vet who also uses conventional medicine. Sister to Joe and Jenny. She has her own laboratory and animal hospital. Partner of Edward a farmer. The path of Val and Edward's relationship has been complicated by the spirit of Sherebar's brother, Derebar. Val is the mother of David Joshua. Edwards son.

Joe

Brother of Jenny and Val, an expert programmer and sometime illegal hacker. Has worked for the government in the past. He has telepathic connection with Jenny and his other sister Val, a vet.

Doug

A doctor with a vision, brought up in the tough area of Bermondsey, South London. Doug met Sherebar when he gave a hypnotherapy talk at Doug's doctors practice.

Ma Taylor

Doug's mentor and adopted mum.

Sally

A scientist, who runs research for a vaccine, at an underground facility with Sherebar. Sally helped to save Doug's life, when he was poisoned by one of Sherebar's science team, during a vaccination trial.

Edward

A Farmer who became a victim of Derebar when he had an accident. He had to watch as Derebar took over his body and relationship with Val. Edward found it difficult to accept what happened, and that the resulting child David Joshua, was his and Val's son.

Josh

The son of Hannah, who runs Val's practice. Josh is telepathic and has abilities that are not yet fully developed.

Marika

A contemporary of Sherebar who helps Jenny, Val, Joe, Sally, Edward, Josh, and Doug when they need sanctuary. She is a calming and clear headed when caught in a crisis.

Buster

Jenny's white Alsatian, who has a mind of his own. He has a telepathic connection with Josh.

Cassie

Val's dog, sister to Buster. She has the same telepathic ability.

Thor

An organisation determined to take over the world. Controlled by the dark elements of some of Sherebar's race.

New Main Characters in Betrayal of the Innocent

Ginny

A girl from the backstreets of London.

Alistair

Helps Val in the Laboratory. Lives in her village. Val and Jenny rescue his mother, father, and sister when Thor used them to blackmail Alistair.

Ella

Alistair's sister.

Lewis

An engineer works with Alister's dad.

Andy

A young boy captured by Thor.

Wilf

A music producer husband of Maggie.

Maggie

Musician and music producer.

The General

Controls what is left of the armed forces.

PREVIOUSLY...

Sherebar lived down the centuries, his love, life, and grief intensified as he is persecuted by Derebar, his malevolent brother's vindictive spirit.

There are three siblings, Jenny a programmer and designer, Joe, a computer hacker who ventures into places he shouldn't go, and Val, a vet with an unusual affinity to animals.

When the siblings come across danger, love, and heart-break, they discover a dark secret that is interwoven with Sherebar's past, which may threaten all their future. Together they are the beacon of hope for the world.

CHAPTER ONE

In an underground bunker a group of sombre men and women watched their worst fears become a reality. A bank of screens showed empty streets, as a shower of debris rained on various parts of the world. One woman could be overheard nervously murmuring to the man next to her, that it wasn't so much the debris she was worried about, but the virus it contained. They all knew the Government had been armed with the knowledge of how deadly it could be for two years. Preparations had been taking place to help those who survived, but the people in the bunker knew it was too little, too late. It was a burden they would have to bare in the coming years as part of that Government.

There had been furious debates about whether they should have warned the population earlier. Everyone in the bunker knew that there hadn't been enough vaccine to go around all the population. Revaccination if needed could be a problem. The vaccine had been more difficult to make than any of the other vaccines produced in the past, even with the Government's enhanced knowledge and the ability to sequence DNA.

They had vaccinated essential services, NHS staff, some food producers, small useful manufacturers, and the military, but a large part of the population would be vulnerable. No one was sure how long the virus would last outside, if anyone was immune, or if there would be pockets of the population around the world who had escaped.

As they watched their screens, the people noticed a group of three young men walking down an empty street, trying doors to see if any were unlocked. Suddenly, one of the three doubled over, bringing up a green liquid that made the others gag, and hold their hands up to cover their faces. Another boy fell over and laid still in the road. The young man that was left, turned, and ran back to a nearby house, hammered on the door and was let in by an older lady, who pulled him in and quickly shut the door. Within minutes a vehicle arrived, and the bodies were removed by two people in hazard suits, who quickly drove away. The question from those watching, was how the remaining young man had survived. This was something they needed to look at, and fast. Was he immune, had he been vaccinated and if so, how?

Two weeks previously, a public warning had circulated throughout the world in all languages, the UK Government had also put out a public service announcement on all social media platforms, the news media, BBC, posters, and every other available means of communication, telling the population, as a precaution, to stay indoors when sirens sounded, and to make sure windows, doors, and chimneys were blocked.

The Government said, fourteen days of food should be stored by all households from the date of this announcement, there were no exceptions. Everyone had to comply. Food parcels would be available to those without the means to buy enough food. There was no need to panic buy they said, as this had been planned for by the government and food stocks were high.

They explained this was a precaution because of an Asteroid collision, meteor air burst and meteor shower expected to hit the earth in two weeks' time. The Government warned people to stay calm, as the situation was under control, but no one, under any circumstances should touch the dust or meteor fragments outside or leave their homes until the all-clear.

The Government announcement continued with conviction, that there were plans in place to keep public order. Hoping to ward off any panic by not admitting that dealing with the possible number of bodies, could be a severe problem.

CHAPTER TWO

Virginia who liked to be called Ginny, was at home when she heard the announcement, and knew the time she had been training for had arrived. She remembered when she first met Sherebar. She had been twelve and a wild child, answering back her teachers, bunking off school, refusing to work, and stealing her mother's alcohol when she could. A big girl with red hair, tall for her age, and usually in second hand un-ironed clothes. Electric for an iron wasn't something felt to be important by her Mum. She'd felt different from the other children in their clean, neat uniforms, and was in danger of falling into the hands of county lines gangs, so prevalent in her area.

She didn't know why she went to Sherebar's talk at school. She thought it may be a laugh. He was commanding, tall, slim, with a shock of long white hair curling on the top of his collar. There was something special about him. No one talked, all listened - even her, such was his command of the room.

When they were leaving without the normal jostling and noise, Sherebar asked four of them to stay behind. They met once a week in a classroom at the school and what she learned changed her life. She found she liked learning what he taught, and never missed a session.

Living in a squalid flat in a dingy high-rise block, up four dirty urine smelling stairways, she looked around the room. Clothes on the floor, unwashed dishes in the sink, and her mother comatose on dirty bedlinen. Drunk or drugged she wasn't sure which. She didn't know who her dad was, or even if he had fathered her siblings Belle and Tip too.

Silently, she went into the bedroom she shared with her ten-year-old sister Bel and twelve-year-old brother Tip, and lifted the floorboards. Hidden under a pile of clothes she took out a backpack, three parcels, money, and travel tickets. Without a backward look she left the untidy flat and headed for the stairs ignoring the litter, as a rancid smell hit her nostrils and made her gag. Her heart sunk when she saw her mother's dealer heading her way. Frantically looking around for somewhere to hide she noticed the door to the bin room was open and slipped inside. She held her breath as he passed, she knew she didn't have much time, as he would come looking for her when he realised her mum was unconscious. It was urgent for her to get out, and she had a feeling she was only just in time. Once in the gangs it was hard to escape and being a girl, she had no illusions as to what would be in store for her, despite her strength and size.

Running to Bels' school, she grabbed her hand as she came out, ignoring Bels querying look. They met Tip at the end of the road. Both knew not to ask questions, used to doing what Ginny said. When a bus came round the corner, stopping at the nearby bus stop, they all jumped on. Two stops before Liverpool Street Station they got off the bus and took the back roads and alleyways. Arriving just in time to catch the Colchester train. Ginny hoped she had done enough to confuse anyone who came looking for her.

The train was crowded with commuters going home, but no one took any notice of this small group. The three of them sat huddled together on one row of seats and didn't speak. The journey took just over an hour, and they came through the station departure gates, showing the tickets Ginny had, without a problem.

'As you've both been so good,' Ginny said, 'we'll find something to eat, but first we need to change.'

'I'm not going into the girls loo,' complained Tip 'I'm too big for that.'

Although Tip was quite slight and could easily have passed as a ten-year-old Ginny didn't want an argument at this stage. 'Look,' she pointed, 'there's a Mac Donald's over there, they have loos, but you go straight to a cubicle, and I'll wait outside. Take too long and I'll come and get you,' she warned, giving him a parcel from her backpack.

When Tip came out dressed in joggers, tee-shirt and carrying a dark green hoodie, she gave him a thumbs up and said. 'Give me those old clothes and find a table. Bel and I won't be long.' They found the disabled toilet, and both went in to change, Bel had joggers, tee-shirt, and hoody like Tip, but in dark blue, Ginny had slim black trousers, long light green top and a black hoody. She also wore a dark green beret that hid her distinctive hair.

'Wow,' said Tip as they approached the table, 'you look great.'

'Shhh,'" warned Ginny, putting her fingers to her lips. 'We don't want to bring notice to ourselves.'

'But I've never seen you looking like that. I'm scared Ginny. Where are we going?' asked Tip his lip quivering.

'We're getting on another train which shouldn't be so crowded, and I promise I'll tell you what I know. Can you wait till then?' asked Ginny gently.

Tip nodded and clutched Ginny's hand, which made her realise how frightened he was.

'Don't worry now,' she said. 'Think of it as an adventure, let's order our food as we don't have much time.'

They ate in silence as they were hungry, so it didn't take long. Ginny taking both their hands, ran with them through the ticket barrier, to the Norwich platform after showing her tickets to the man at the gate. (Which was open as the ticket barrier had broken down) and got on the waiting train.

The carriage was half empty and they sat together far away from listening ears. It looked as if people were staying at home already.

'Come close,' Ginny said putting her arms round Tip and Bel. Something Tip wouldn't normally allow and began her story. 'A man called Sherebar came to our school to give a talk about science and asked four of us to stay behind,' said Ginny. Realising she was responsible for Tip and Bel now.

'What a funny name,' interrupted Tip.

'Do you want to hear the story or not?' snapped Ginny and was immediately sorry, as she saw his eyes water. 'I didn't mean to snap Tip. I'm only tired as I didn't get much sleep last night, shall I carry on?' Tip nodded and moved closer.

'Sherebar taught me a lot.' she continued. 'I learnt to use my mind to protect myself,' (*and you two*) she hoped. 'I learnt martial arts, like Judo, how to programme, and research. He told us he had arrived from far away and his people loved our world, but they knew there would be a problem in the future. They had to wait until the earth's population had advanced enough to be able to use the help and technology his people offered. He told us he had lived through several of our lifetimes and had lost dearly loved family. Do you understand what I'm saying?' She quietly asked Bel and Tip.

'I think so,' answered Tip. 'Was he a spaceman?'

I'm not sure,' said Ginny smiling, 'but he was so interesting, and taught me a lot. He told me I had to be ready to leave home at short notice.' Not that I minded that she thought, seeing the picture of her mum slumped drunk on the bed, in her head, 'and that someone called Josh would tell me when.'

'I said I wouldn't come without you two, and I asked why I needed to leave home, and he showed me in pictures in my mind about a virus making everyone ill and told me that I needed to go to somewhere safe. He gave me the clothes we're wearing, money, and tickets for me to keep until we needed it. I had to make sure they were hidden from Mum.'

'What's a virus, and do you trust him?' asked Tip nervously, 'and how do you know where to go?'

'A virus makes you ill, and yes, I trust him. It's difficult to explain why,' explained Ginny. 'I've known him for two years now and he's helped me cope better with home. Today Josh has been talking to me in my mind, and he tells me where to go next. It's like a sat-nav in your mind. We'll meet him soon; He's coming to meet us with someone called Val who's a Vet, and a dog called Cassie.' Looking down at Bel Ginny asked, 'are you okay, you're quiet?'

'Will we all stay together?' Bel asked in a subdued voice, 'cause I'm afraid to be on my own.'

'We will all stay together don't worry,' confirmed Ginny firmly. 'I wouldn't leave you ever. I promise.'

Ginny knew life was going to be quite different for the three of them but didn't regret taking them on this journey one bit. Life was difficult at home coping with her mum and not knowing where the next pound was coming from. Dodging the drug dealers and gangs, knowing that Bel and Tip could be the next victims. A sad fact in the area they grew up in.

She could fight for herself now but hadn't been tested yet, so she didn't regret anything. What was coming could come.

She would deal with it. She thought *I'm not a redhead for nothing* and had learnt over the past two years to (mostly) channel her anger at the world more constructively. It would be a new kind of life but couldn't be worse than the one they'd left, could it?

CHAPTER THREE

Bel had fallen asleep her head on Ginny's lap. As the train slowed down to a stop at the Norwich platform Ginny gently woke her up and said. 'Come on time to go.' She took Bel's hand gave Tip a nudge before they jumped off the train.

'Where to now?' asked Tip a bit overwhelmed. Ginny guessed it was because he hadn't been this far from London before.

'We go down here and out by the river,' answered Ginny with a bit more confidence than she felt. 'Josh should be along the road somewhere.' Dusk was falling and it was making her a bit jittery. She didn't know the area and felt increasingly unsettled.

Walking towards them was a tall woman with long blond hair and a confident stride, with a big white Alsatian on a lead. Ginny felt a calmness infusing her body and instinctively knew that this was Val who they were expecting to meet with Josh. Val stopped and the dog sat, as they waited for the tired looking little group to reach them.

'Hi, I'm Val' she said gently, 'and this is Cassie,' indicating the dog who immediately held up her paw to Bel. who fell completely in love. 'Would you hold her for me?' Val asked Bel, giving her the lead with a smile.

'Me?' asked Bel with a gasp of delight, as Cassie proceeded to lick her hand.

Val turned to Ginny, thinking how brave this prickly young woman was. Coming all this way, looking after her siblings, and trusting Sherebar so completely that she embarked on this journey into the unknown. Putting her arms round her to give her a hug, Val felt Ginny stiffen and realised she would have to take it slowly to gain her trust. Letting her arms drop she turned to Tip and said. 'I know this is all strange to you, but you're safe now. You look tired so I think I should get you home, where you can have something to eat. Is that ok with you?'

Tip looked at the ground but nodded his agreement.

Val sensed that he had decided that she must be safe if Ginny had accepted her.

They walked to a waiting People Carrier and Val suggested Bel sat in the back with Cassie. Bel looked like she was in heaven as Cassie moved closer and proceeded to lick her face with enthusiasm, 'I've never been allowed a dog at home and this one seems to like me,' she laughed putting her arms round Cassie.

'I know you've communicated for months but I'm sure you'll have a lot to talk about with Josh, now that you can meet.' Val said with a smile as she opened the door. 'Josh look who's here at last, move up so Ginny can get in.'

'This is surreal,' said Ginny. "I never expected this to happen'.

'You'll see a lot of stranger things before this is finished,' grinned Josh. 'Happy you made it, and my directions were clear enough. Mum's laying on a feast, so we better start home, she thought you would be hungry after a stressful journey.' Ginny felt a wave of longing for a mum who made her a feast. The last vision of her mum wasn't one she wanted to remember.

'Tip, you sit in the front with me, and you can tell me all about the adventure you've had.' Said Val as she started the car for the long drive home.

Ginny watched the fields roll by, she'd never seen so many, or any cows and sheep. This was a whole new world. Well, she thought to herself *it can't be worse than where we came from, can it?* Eventually they drew up by a wooden gate, Val got out of the car, opened it, and drove a short way to what Ginny thought was the most beautiful house she had ever seen. It was long and low with windows in the roof. There were roses around the door that left a strong scent in the evening air. Chickens and ducks wandered around, and a horse looked enquiringly out of a nearby stable.

The front door was opened by a small woman with short curly hair, in jeans, a vibrantly coloured top, and a big smile. A dog was jumping around her feet. She stood with open arms to give Josh a hug.

'Hi Mum 'Josh said. 'This is Ginny, Bel and Tip.'

'Welcome,' said Hannah, Josh's mum. 'Come in, I expect you are tired and hungry, why don't you show them their rooms Josh, while I get the food ready.'

'Are you coming in Val?' Hannah enquired.

'No, but I'll be back in the morning, I need to get back to my son as Edward's been looking after him. Edward needs to check everything is working ok in the farm. We don't have much time left. To say it will be bad is an understatement. I'm trying to be positive, and I know we've put in place as much as we can here, but I can't help wondering if there's more we could have done.'

Val turned to Ginny, and said, 'You're in safe hands, I know it is quite different for you all, but Josh will explain what's happening and we will talk tomorrow.' She didn't try to give them a hug this time, and Ginny guessed she'd realised the big change that day, was a little overwhelming for them all.

'Come on,' said Josh 'I'll show you your rooms and explain a bit about what's happening, then we'll eat.'

Ginny, Bel, and Tip trailed behind Josh, gazing around at their surroundings. The hall was large with white-washed walls with red stone floors. Everywhere looked so clean. There were small windows with large windowsills big enough to sit on. Upstairs had views of trees and fields of yellow stuff.

The landing had polished floors and rugs in colours of the rainbow, there were pictures on the walls in pastel colours of the farm, and its animals. Josh took them into a room with a double bed, wardrobe, and its own bathroom. There were thick carpets on the floor and a desk with a computer and game consul. 'This is yours Tip,' said Josh. 'Do you want to look around or come to see Ginny and Bels room?'

'Is this all for me?' Tip asked in amazement.

'Yes,' said Josh with a grin 'I wanted you all near me and we have lots of room here. There will be other children coming to a block we have ready, and I need you all to help me, Is that okay?'

Tip nodded his jaw dropping. In his short life he had never seen a room like it.

Ginny was unusually quiet as she entered the room Josh showed her for her and Bel. She wasn't sure what she expected, but it was nothing like this. It was all a bit overwhelming. The room was large with an adjoining room for Bel they had a shared bathroom and a settee with two plump chairs.

It was vibrant and full of colour. There was a desk, a

computer, a bookcase with lots of books, and a window that opened onto a view of a garden. Suddenly Ginny sat down on the bed tears streaming from her eyes. She'd never had a room to herself before.

'What's the matter?' asked Josh with concern in his voice, 'don't you like it.'

'Of course I do,' said Ginny between sobs, but why are you doing this? You don't know us. What's the catch? Nothing comes free in this world, in my experience.'

Josh seemed like he wasn't sure what to do, then he heard Val's calm voice in his head. She said, 'talk to her Josh. Tell her your story, they all need to know, as we are all in this together.'

CHAPTER FOUR

Josh sat on the bed beside Ginny, Tip and Bel sat on the floor.

'I do know about tough times Ginny,' Josh said. 'Mum and I didn't always live like this, although the farm was always ours. My Dad was a soldier, he left the army to be with us, I loved him so much, he was such fun, but one day he went to the town after a call that upset him.' He rubbed his forehead and frowned in concentration.

'On the way back, Dad was run over by a hit and run driver and died. Mum and I didn't think it was an accident. We thought it was deliberate, but no one believed us, and no one was caught.' Tears sprung to his eyes at the memory, and he brushed them away, but Ginny had already seen them.

'Mum struggled to manage the farm on her own, it was too big for one person, and it got a bit run down. Money was a problem. We couldn't afford help, so she worked for Val at the vets' part time for extra money.'

Josh paused as he found himself shaking with the emotion he still felt as he remembered his dad. He continued. 'Then Matt arrived one day. He said he'd been a friend of

Dads from the army, and when he heard what happened to Dad he wanted to help.'

'Matt helped with the farm and made life easier for Mum. It became that she couldn't manage without him. I didn't like him much, in fact I hated him, there was something about him I didn't trust, but when Matt asked Mum to marry him, she agreed.' Josh walked to look out of the window, taking a big breath to calm himself down.

'I didn't say anything as mum seemed happy and I was young. It didn't take long for him to change though. He drank, didn't work, and hit Mum all the time. I was too small to help her, and he made my life a misery. He shot the dog my Dad gave me, and took all Mums money that she earnt at the vets.'

Ginny gasped in horror as Josh continued the story he was telling.

'He thought he could take over the farm too, but dad had left it, and any money in Trust for me, that's why the farm was run down. So, Matt couldn't mortgage it or borrow money against it, and if anything happened to me, it went to a distant cousin. Dad changed his will just before he died. We're not sure why.'

Josh moved back to sit by Ginny, the closeness to her comforting. Unusually she didn't move away as this would have been her normal reaction.

'We were often hungry, but Mum was too scared to leave or tell anyone. Matt took my pet rat Dooley, who listened and comforted me when I was scared. I could tell her my worries and she could read my mind. He took her to a research laboratory to spite me and hit me so hard when I tried to stop him, that I passed out.'

Ginny gave Josh's arm a squeeze, he turned to look at her in surprise, and she gave him a small smile of encouragement

'Mum found me and wanted to take me to hospital, but I

refused so she took me to Val's. Val sorted my head wound and she helped me rescue Dooley and a little dog called Toby. The one you see running around causing havoc outside.'

'On the way home, Val and I saw Matt's car. I was so scared that he'd see me, but he'd hit a tree while drunk and died. It was such a relief, and I was happy he'd gone, he deserved to die for what he did to my Mum. It got better then.'

'I'm sorry it was so hard for you Josh,' said Ginny with concern.

'What happened next?'

Looking at their earnest faces, Josh continued. 'Mum took over managing the Vet Practice and the research lab, where Val makes her medicines. So, we had more money.' Said Josh as the memories came back.

'Val arranged for her partner Edward's father, to run our farm. He lives here now. He's brilliant, Mum loves him, and he loves us both. He helped to sort the house, so don't think things can't get better.'

'Sherebar believes in you, or you wouldn't be here. You've met him and know how amazing he is. It's going to get quite hairy in the next two weeks which is why Sherebar wanted you to come and stay with us now, it's safer. He was impressed with you and knew you had abilities that only a few of us have.'

Ginny was teary and wide eyed. This was a lot to take in and her bones ached with the effort of the day.

Josh spoke again, his voice full of emotion.

'Val has these abilities too, so do her sister Jenny, and brother Joe. You'll like him. He's a brilliant hacker and programmer, plus he's good fun.'

'The world is going to be hit by a virus soon. You heard the governments message, didn't you? and it's safer here. I'll tell you more about it later, you're getting tired, are you hungry? Let's find food,' continued Josh, pulling Ginny to her feet.

'Yes', said Tip jumping up. I'm starving.'

'So am I,' piped up Bel finding her voice at last. 'Are we having toast.'

'With beans if you're lucky.' laughed Ginny drying her tears and trying to take in all Josh had told her. She'd reserve judgement for the moment and see what happened next.

They all sat round a table. This is another new experience, realised Ginny as she sat down. The three of them had never sat at a table for food except at school, lucky for them they'd had free school meals. Food was scarce at home. *They'll have to take us as we are*. Thought Ginny grimly.

Hannah brought in plates of big fat sausages, piles of chips and beans.

She said with a smile, 'I wasn't sure what you would like so I thought I would keep it simple this time,' and didn't understand when Josh and Ginny burst out laughing.

The atmosphere suddenly felt lighter to Ginny. She could see that Tip, and Bel couldn't believe their eyes when chocolate cake and ice cream came next.

When they had all finished their meal, Hannah called out from the kitchen. 'How about you all have a look round outside, then go and watch TV, or read for a while, as I know you must be tired '.

'Can I see the horse,' piped up Bel. 'I've never seen a real one before.'

'I'll take you if you can wait a minute,' said Hannah. 'Is that okay with you?' she asked Ginny.

'I'll wait in my room,' replied Ginny, thinking she'd had enough happy families for today, but admitting to herself she was jealous.

She felt a gentle probe in her mind, as if someone was trying to read her thoughts, and turned to Josh furiously, 'don't do that, my thoughts are private,' and stormed up the stairs.

Josh followed her and knocked on her door.

'Go away,' she said, 'I don't want to talk to you.'

'I'm sorry,' said Josh through the door. 'You seemed sad. I should have asked you first about connecting with our minds. I was curious. I promise I won't do it again.'

'Come in then, but if you do it again, you'll be sorry. Does your Mum have the same talent?' asked Ginny.' I need to be ready if she does.'

'No, Val, Jenny, and Joe do, but they can all block their minds. We keep it to ourselves. Mum doesn't know, she'd be worried all the time if she did.'

'I want you to be here Ginny. It's going to get scary and Sherebar thought we could be friends and help each other through this. They need our skills. Can we be friends?' asked Josh.

'I'll think about it,' said Ginny a bit huffily. She still hadn't forgiven him for being able to read her mind so easily. 'I think you should go now; can you send Bel up when she's had enough of the animals, I'm tired and there is a lot to think about.'

CHAPTER FIVE

The next morning Ginny woke up and for a minute didn't know where she was. This must be like one of those swanky hotels she thought not believing her luck. Why was she here, she wondered. What would it mean for her, Bel, and Tip? Looking at the clock on the wall, she realised never in her life had any of them slept undisturbed for so long, or without the fear that her mother had brought home some druggie or drunk, they would have to dodge before going to school.

Ginny heard a noise coming from Bels' room and Bel came through the door rubbing her eyes. She had a night dress on. *Another first thought* Ginny. *I wonder where she got that?* Not having thought to look in any cupboards or drawers herself.

'You okay Bel?' enquired Ginny.

'I like it here Ginny,' Bel replied in a shaky voice. 'Do you think they'll let us stay? I could help with the animals.'

'I don't know Bel,' said Ginny, pulling Bel to her to give her a hug.

'Let's find Tip and go downstairs to see if there's any food and I'll ask.'

'Go put some clothes on, I'm starving.'

When they were both dressed, (Ginny having slept in her tee shirt) they quietly left the room and went next door to Tips room. Opening the door without knocking, as at home they all slept in one room. Privacy wasn't something they were used to, they found Tip curled up and still fast asleep.

'We'll leave him, he was so tired last night,' whispered Ginny taking Bel's hand, 'let's find some food.'

On the kitchen table there were cereal's, warm rolls, butter, jam and bananas, glasses of orange juice and a hand-written note that said, help yourself to anything you want. I am outside feeding the horse. Val will be here at 10am to take Ginny and Josh to a meeting. Bel and Tip can stay with me, I'll show them the farm if that's OK? Hannah x.

What if I don't want to go to a meeting Ginny thought rebelliously. Then she reminded herself that this was serious, and no one knew what it was going to be like, so she needed to go along with this change in their life for the moment. it was safer than home. She had to survive for Bel and Tip.

Just as they were finishing breakfast Hannah came in and asked, 'Bel would you like to collect the eggs with me this morning?' Bel looked at Ginny to see if it would be ok.

Ginny nodded. 'That's fine,' she said, 'but I need to know what's happening with us. Are we staying here? Why are we here and what's going on? I'd like the truth.'

Hannah sighed. 'The world is going to change Ginny, and it will be devastating,' she said. 'Sherebar, a friend of Val's and Josh, sent you here as you were a pen friend of Josh, and it's a safer place to be. He was worried about you. You were his best student from the school he helped in, and Josh explained your situation to me. The world is going to need young people like you and Josh to survive. Sherebar also felt a connection to you. The same as he has with Josh.'

She continued as she busied herself gathering up the egg boxes, for Bel. 'There will be those who want to take what we have here so we must be ready. Everyone will need to know what to do to protect themselves. There is an organisation called Thor that wants the knowledge we've gathered.'

'Go to the meeting, Val will explain,' she said kindly. 'You are all welcome here this is your home if you want to stay. It will be lovely to have youngsters around again. Josh is growing up so fast.'

CHAPTER SIX

The village hall was packed with villagers. One adult from each household in the village had been asked to attend, and it looked to Val as if most had come. The noise levels were so high. It was important for their survival that the village worked together. She hoped they could all agree.

Val could feel that the atmosphere was tense, people were worried, not knowing what to expect. The population had been told to stay at home by the Government, so why was Val so insistent everyone came to this meeting? She had to give them the answers.

Val took to the stage and asked for quiet so she could begin. She was tall and had the charisma of someone confident in her abilities. Edward her partner and a farmer, (who was trying to make sure the village had the food it would need), looked on with admiration at her poise and passion. They had been through a lot of traumas over the last year and were just trying to put their life back together again.

'You all know me well,' she said 'Edward and I love this village and as you know from the Governments broadcast, there is the probability that a meteor shower will hit the earth in about twelve days' time. What they didn't tell you was that the meteor shower, and the dust that comes with it, carry a virus that is deadly if you breath or touch it.' A murmur of worry flowed through the room.

'There's no cure and if you haven't been vaccinated or are naturally immune, you will die. Sorry to be so blunt but that's the truth. I and several others across the world, have been working in our labs to try and find a vaccine in time.'

People gasped and a couple began sobbing quietly.

Val continued. 'The Government has also been working on this, and a vaccine that worked has been given to as many people as possible, but there is not enough for everyone.'

At this point there was an uproar in the room as some villagers stood up and demanded more information.

'Please hear me out,' said Val holding up her hand for silence.

'Dr Foster who you all know well has been vaccinating everyone here who accepted a flu jab, as we couldn't spread panic by explaining the addition of the new vaccine. The Government hadn't told the public the truth, and we didn't want to cause a riot'. Knowing the audience was getting restive she quickly continued.

'All children under ten who have had a measles vaccine are also covered. This new vaccine addition to the measles jab for children, didn't work on adults and they still don't know why. Unfortunately, some children were not immunised, and they will be at risk.'

She looked around and saw a sea of faces blurring into each other, as her tension mounted, her body was getting warm, and perspiration was beginning to make her uncomfortable. Taking a big breath, she continued

'As most of you know, my sister Jenny and her partner Doug, who is a doctor and nearly died testing the new vaccine, have moved here for the foreseeable future. Doug will be joining Dr Foster in his practice. Any child who has not had a measles vaccination or is over ten and any adult who hasn't had the modified flu vaccination from Dr Foster should see the doctors today.'

'There is not much time, and this is extremely important. If you are not vaccinated, you are at risk,' said Val her body beginning to shake with anxiety. Flinging her arms wide in a gesture to encompass them all, she continued.

'The village is protected; I will explain in more detail later when we have more time. We have our own electricity, water, communication hubs, transport, food storage and sewerage. Something we have been working on for the last two years, with the help of a man called Sherebar, a friend and scientist. He has the knowledge that has helped us to prepare for the disaster coming. There will also be limited Wi-Fi, as many communications networks will be down.' (Val didn't want to point out the true extent of this now.)

'We have farms, a working Mill, and have been actively attracting the crafts we think we will need. Unfortunately there will be those who want to take what we have, and there will be children without parents that we want to save. Are you prepared to fight for what we have, for it may come to that? We will continue to make the vaccine as we don't yet know how long the virus will be around for, or how long a vaccination protection will last. You may all need boosters, and surviving this together is our aim.' Taking a deep breath to steady her nerves she continued.

'Although desperate times are now upon us, there are several positives in our situation, there are also minuses that I'm sure you will think of, but for now I need you to trust me and those I work with. I know it's a lot to ask but the reality is, if we want to survive, we must work together. I will answer some questions now and we will have some smaller workshops in the next week.'

'Why didn't you tell us before?' shouted an angry villager. 'We could have been better prepared if we had known? Who's this Sherebar? 'Why did you vaccinate this village, what will happen to our families not living here?'

'How do we protect ourselves?' queried another agitated villager, as others murmured their agreement.

*This is going to be diffi*cult thought Val to herself as she prepared to answer some awkward questions. Taking a big breath, she began.

'I had a usable laboratory here; the vaccine is not as easy to produce as others have been in the past. Despite our advance knowledge it takes more time than usual to make. We didn't have a large supply, and we didn't know for some time if it would work. If we had told you, however much we all here wanted to keep it a secret, it would have got out that we had a store of the vaccine.' Looking around she just saw a sea of hostile faces, taking a deep breath to calm her nerves she continued. 'This would have made us a target for Thor, a criminal organisation that wants to control the supply, Thor will try to take our vaccine from us. They've already tried more than once; we can't let that happen; it's needed here. Or the Government would want to confiscate it to add to their own inadequate stock. I know most of you by name, I've lived in this village a long time, and during the past two years, those working with me have made sure the village is self-sufficient in most things we need to survive,' said Val with quiet conviction. 'Vaccinating you all was a feasible target because of the villages size, and without doing this, all of us would be way down the list of those chosen to receive the vaccination from bureaucrats in charge. I was insistent that if we made the vaccine here, you in my village would be first to get it. As for who is Sherebar, that's more difficult for me to answer, as it will sound like science fiction' It will take a leap of faith for some of you to believe what I am going to tell you. I will try to simplify the story please listen before making any judgments.'

In a voice calmer than she felt possible, Val took a deep breath and began.' Centuries ago, a group of advanced beings, including Sherebar, lived on earth. Their technology was advanced and can seem magical. Some of them decided to stay when their island was destroyed. They knew this virus was coming, and that their help would be needed in the future. They lived through the centuries until the time their knowledge could be used, and we had the technology to implement it.'

Someone in the audience laughed, 'you're right about a fairy story.'

Another said, 'shush let's hear Val out.'

Getting increasingly agitated and having trouble containing it, Val related the rest of her story. 'Their descendants throughout the world are immune to the virus, but we don't know how many of them there are. My sister, brother and I didn't realise we are part of this immune group, or that this would enable us to help, until a meeting with Sherebar a few years ago. Even Sherebar and those like him have their limits, so are helping those best able to survive throughout the world.'

'As for family members not living here, that's a difficult one. Unusually this village has several families with three generations already living here. Partly due to the provision of jobs, and creative vision of the village. We also have young families and a lot of talent. We can't accommodate everyone but if anyone has immediate family and we have room to house them come and talk to me after this.'

The villagers were getting restive, this was a lot to take in for them, and Val had a problem in making herself heard.

Raising her voice, she said. 'Travel is difficult and the survival of those here is a priority for me. Phone calls and communication out of the village is banned for your own safety for the moment, as we cannot alert outside forces to our situation.'

There was uproar at this, 'who are you to tell us what to do?' shouted one.

'Why should we believe you?' shouted another.

Val looked around helplessly, she had hoped that as they knew her, they would trust her, but this looked as if it could get out of hand. She wasn't sure what to do. Then suddenly there was a hush as a man appeared on the stage as if by magic. His presence commanded attention and the commotion in the room ceased. It was eerily quiet.

'I am Sherebar,' he announced. He seemed to grow in stature with every word. The atmosphere electric. 'Do you want to live?' he asked angrily. 'Do you realise the love, tears and even death it has cost to get this far? Why have I lived all this time for an ungrateful world when I could have left you to your fate? I will help you survive but you need to realise you have to play your part.'

The villagers were mesmerised as he continued.

'Val insisted that you villagers be given the vaccine she produced, first, this is her home and she wanted to protect you all. The whole world will be changed, and nature needs to be given time to rejuvenate, you can be part of it, but you can also leave tonight if you wish to do so. and take your chance with the rest of the world. What is it to be?' Are you going to support Val or not?'

A young woman stood up. 'I support Val,' she said. 'I trust her more than local bureaucrats, they haven't vaccinated any of us, have they? They would have left us to die. Why would she tell us this if it wasn't true? I know it sounds like a fantasy, but I don't want to take a chance. Tell us what we need to do to keep our families safe Val, I'm with you.'

Someone started clapping and shouted,' I'm with you too Val,' and gradually everyone except one man joined in. He got up and left. Sherebar nodded to someone nearby and he followed the man out. Sherebar turned to Val, smiled, and without another word, left to join his companion, who had followed the villager, as he left the meeting.

CHAPTER SEVEN

'Hallo Midra' said Sherebar as he and his companion confronted the man. 'I wondered what'd happened to you, I won't let you control this village or steal Val and Edwards child, he will grow up here in safety. His power is yet unknown and will not be of use to you.'

The man called Midra smiled. 'You can't stop me Sherebar, I have as much power as you, I'm surprised you didn't realise I was here before, too busy elsewhere I expect. Derebar did an excellent job protecting this village but not good enough. I found a trace and was welcomed here. I didn't expect your malevolent twin to help in this way. It wasn't something to do with the child, was it?' He said watching Sherebar closely before resuming. 'The village will live, just not in the way they expected. This race is inferior, look at the damage they have done to the world. The child will fulfil the prophecy in their religious books, join me and with him, we will rule this world,'

'Our purpose was not to rule this world Midra, it was to nurture and help when the time was right,' reminded Sherebar. 'Our Island was destroyed to remind us of that. The child David Joshua stays here with his mother Val, do not try to take him, he has my, and despite his bad reputation, Delabar's protection too.' With that a beam of light went from both Sherebar and his companion past Midra's mind protection and erased all his memory of the village and child.

Midra rolled on the floor and his body stilled.

'Take him to Marika,' said Sherebar to his companion. 'Without your help I would've had a problem. He was strong and had protected his mind well. I should have detected him sooner. I just hope Marika, (who was one of Sherebar's race, and had helped Val, and her siblings in the past), and her sanctuary can help him realise our true purpose, or we could have more problems in the future.'

Silently a black car drew up beside them and they carried the prone body to the car. Touching fingers, they said good-bye. The companion got in, and the car left as silently as it'd arrived.

Sherebar was just returning to the hall, when he heard a voice call 'Sherebar,' as Josh ran to him with Ginny to tow, a big smile on his face.' I knew you'd come and help Val,' he said jumping up and down with excitement. 'Ginny arrived with her brother and sister, they're staying with us, we're going to help Joe with communications and other things,' he said with a grin.

'This is serious Josh. Not a game,' remonstrated Sherebar. Although he privately thought that Jenny and Val's brother Joe, who worked at Sherebar's underground facility and laboratory, was an expert programmer, and sometime hacker, often thought the 'other things' were fun too.

'How are you feeling Ginny?' enquired Sherebar turning to her.

'It's a bit strange,' said Ginny suddenly feeling a bit shy. *Another new feeling,* she thought. 'Whatever happens I would rather be here than at home. It's safer for Bel and Tip, they like it here. Bels found a love of animals, and Tip of machines. He's always to be found under a tractor, often covered in oil, to the despair of Hannah.'

'This is the right place for you Ginny.' said Sherebar with a smile. 'You and Josh will be powerful together. Don't ever forget that in the time ahead. I'm going to talk to Val and Edward now but will see to you both before I go.' With that he walked back into the hall.

CHAPTER EIGHT

Val was talking to one of the older villagers, surprisingly the only one who had asked to bring extra family members to the village. Her girls had grown up in the village she said, but they moved out with their husband's jobs. That showed, Val said to herself, that their decision to try and bring whole family units to the village, when employing anyone in the last two years, had worked.

As Sherebar joined them, Val introduced the villager. 'Can we bring Mrs Upton's family here. She has two daughters and three grandchildren, twelve, fourteen, and sixteen. They live just two hours away.'

'What do their partners do,' asked Sherebar. 'They would have to come tonight. Do you think they would leave everything?'

'My youngest daughter's husband is an engineer, and she works in a local bank. The other runs her own dressmaking business and her husbands a baker,' said Mrs Upton. 'They live near each other. When I tell them how serious this is, I'm sure they'll come.' Mrs Upton's eyes darted round the room, and Val could see she was pleading with her fellow villagers for approval.

'That would work,' said Val. 'We could do with an engineer at the Mill, and we don't have a baker in the village. A dressmaker would be good too. We have a local artisan who, weaves the sheep and alpaca wool. She's been good at attracting tourists her cloth is so good.' Not that there will be any tourists now, she mused.

'Speak to them now,' advised Sherebar, handing Mrs Upton a secure mobile, phone, specially programmed by Joe for emergencies, 'but warn them not to tell anyone what they are doing. You can explain this is serious and for their own safety, but they will have to trust you and come tonight. They will be picked up in three hours exactly and notified of the rendezvous in two and a half hours. Tell them to wear dark clothing if they have any, and only bring one back- pack each. Anything they will need when here, will be provided.'

Mrs Upton rushed off to telephone them.

'Do you think they'll come?' Asked Val.

'I don't know,' answered Sherebar. 'But if they notify the authorities, we could be in trouble.'

CHAPTER NINE

Thirty minutes later Doug and Edward were driving to the rendezvous, Val having taken over Doug's vaccination duties. They arrived dead on time without a problem at a disused airfield Hanger. A group of seven people were waiting for them in the darkness.

Edward got out and opened the back of the vehicle. 'Do you have your passports?' he asked.

One of the men stepped forward and held them out for Edward to check.

No one spoke until one of the teenagers asked, 'what's happening? Why all the cloak and dagger stuff?'

'I'll explain when we get to your Grandma's' Edward said, 'but for now you must be incredibly quiet, and not make a sound if we get stopped. It's a matter of life or death and I'm afraid you will just have to trust us. It's important for your own safety that you do.'

'Supposing you are kidnappers, why should we trust you? How do we know Grandma sent you?' queried the teenager with a scowl.

'Your Grandma said to tell you she has taggy, and you

would know what she meant. Now get in, we don't have much time. Sit on the cushions on the floor, sorry there are no seats.' The group were a bit bemused, but worried enough to do as they were told. 'If we're stopped hide under the rugs.' Said Edward abruptly, having no time for more explanations.

'Mum told us what was happening as we weren't going to come,' said one of the women breaking the silence. 'She told us not to tell you we knew, as someone called Sherebar asked her not to. But she was scared for us and worried we wouldn't come. To be honest we're a bit shell shocked and alarmed. We'll be quiet, don't worry.'

'Ok' said Edward, 'we need to get going.'

Edward put on a blue hazard suit and face mask that Doug handed him before getting back in the vehicle and they were off.

The first part of the journey was uneventful but as they neared the junction there was a roadblock.

'Just what we need,' groaned Doug as he slowed down.

The police officer motioned them to stop and indicated Doug to lower his window. 'Don't come too near officer.' Doug said as he indicated his hazard suit. 'We have contaminated material on board. Please don't touch the side of the ambulance. It may be contaminated.'

The police officer stepped quickly away. They had been warned that there could be more ambulances and mortuary vans on the roads soon.

'Do you have ID?' asked the police officer.

'Yes', said Doug as he flashed the one Sherebar had given him. Don't touch as you don't have gloves on.' They heaved a sigh of relief as they were waved on, and the barriers moved so that they could get by. It was pitch black when they arrived at the Mill House.

'Molly,' said Edward to one of Mrs Upton's daughters, as he opened the back of the van and helped her family out.

'You'll all be tired, I'll leave you to settle in, and will be round in the morning to see if you have everything you need. We will all meet up at 12 o'clock. There is food in the fridge and the bedrooms are ready.'

The weary travellers got out of the van and stretched their legs. Walking towards the door Edward continued 'Here are the keys, we decided as it was so late, we would leave the explaining until tomorrow. If you do want to contact your mum, there is a secure phone inside. Mobiles won't work here for the moment. '

He waited until the family were in the house, and then said to the other daughter, 'we'll take you to the bakery now. The bedrooms are upstairs but there is a kitchen and lounge behind the Bakery downstairs.'

They drove the short distance to the winding High Street, peppered with small shops, and stopped outside a quaint shop next to a greengrocer. Edward opened the doors of the shop and said to Tara as they got out of the van. 'Your Mum will be round in the morning but don't rush to get up. We'll meet tomorrow with me, or Val my partner to explain everything. See you then. If you do want to talk to your mum, use the secure phone inside,' said Edward, as he gave Tara the keys. 'They stick a bit but should be fine to lock up.'

When they walked in Tara's husband switched on the light and looked round. The shop was small but well laid out, room for stacks of bread and a counter display for buns and cakes, a coffee machine and bench with stools. *Would there still be coffee?* He thought. That was a question no one knew the answer to. He'd heard of Acorn coffee but what would that taste like and how did you make it. Not a bit like your usual flat white. Tea? another question although he had tried some grown in England that tasted okay, it was anyone's guess if that would be still available.

Looking around there was a glass wall through which customers could see what was happening in the modern gleaming kitchen.

'Wow,' said Tim. 'This is miles better than anything I'm used to, let's see what the rest is like, it's surreal that it takes a situation like this for me to have my own bakery.'

They went through a door into and open plan area with a kitchen, dining area and comfortable seating. The fourteen-year-old, not looking impressed, until they opened another door to a small room, with a computer, large screen, and a stack of games. Their teenage son gazed around, and his eyes lit up when he saw all the equipment.

'A bit more to your taste Billy?' queried his dad. 'This place is like a Tardis.'

After checking the bedrooms, finding pizzas in the fridge, and feeling a bit more optimistic. They decided to eat and go to bed.

The village has changed a lot in the last two years, Tara said to herself as she went up the stairs. I should have visited Mum here more rather than her coming to us. It looks as if we've landed on our feet in spite of the situation, we're in.

CHAPTER TEN

The next morning Val arranged to meet Mrs Upton and her family at Mrs Upton's house at mid-day, as Edward was busy catching up on all that had to be arranged for the coming onslaught of the problems he anticipated in the future. She was concerned about the time she was spending away from her practice and the vaccine production but realised she had to trust her team. She wanted to get back to being a fulltime vet. That was her love, but looking after a toddler who was growing fast and knowing she would have to sort out her relationship with Edward before too long, was taking its toll. She was in a constant state of stress and knew she was getting grumpy with everyone.

She understood why Edward wanted them to all move to his farmhouse as he felt it was safer, but Val resisted and wanted to stay in her own home for the time being. He had hurt her badly in rejecting his son when he was born, and although Edward had changed now and wanted them to be a family, there was that little bit of her that was still wary. She knew she loved him but was it enough?

Doug, Jenny, and Doug's adoptive mother, Mrs Taylor, were staying with her for the time being, although Doug and Jenny would be moving in with Dr Foster to help run his practice, Jenny was helping teach Tech to the older children, as Joe was adamant that some of the services everyone was used to would still be available, if you were trained to use it. The satellites and other means of communication still being there.

It was lovely having them with her, but she knew they had to move on. Doug was desperately needed by the practice. His wide experience was going to be useful, as there were no hospitals with staff near. Dr Foster an old community style doctor had years of experience of country medicine but was not equipped to deal with major trauma.

There would be a lot of uncertainty around, once the meteor hit. Val was hoping Mrs Taylor, would stay on to help with David Joshua. If not, she would have to find someone to help with him. She had to work, even in this situation, animals still got ill. This was not how she had envisioned her life. She was scared, very scared she admitted to herself, and not being able to admit it to anyone was a strain. 'I'll talk to Edward tonight, 'she said to herself as she went to find Mrs Taylor. She found them in the kitchen, Cassie, and David Joshua both sitting on the floor, looking up at Mrs Taylor expectantly.

Val burst out laughing and felt the tension draining from her. 'What are you two doing,' she said as she picked up her son for a cuddle. 'Cassie have you been leading him astray again, or was it David Joshua leading you?'

Her son's small arms went round her neck as she cuddled him, feeling his warm body against her. The love she felt for him welled up inside making her realise she would do anything for him, and she had to find a way to spend more time with him. Hiding her emotion, she bent down to give Cassie a pat. Who immediately rolled over for a tummy rub.

'Shall I make a cup of tea?' asked Mrs Taylor, 'these two rascals decided to hide in the broom cupboard then couldn't get out. David Joshua is growing, talking, and moving extremely fast for his age.'

Neither of them noticed the little smile he gave. *You have no idea he* thought. Cassie knew, but she wouldn't tell.

'I wanted to talk to you if you have time Mrs Taylor, shall we sit down as I want to put a proposition to you.' Said Val.

'How would you feel at calling me Ma, as Jenny and Doug do?' Said Mrs Taylor with a smile. You have made me so welcome and part of your family, Doug is like a son to me, and I already love these two troublemakers.'

Val was close to tears to have this lady wanting her to be part of her life and realising how much she missed her Mum and Dad, who had died many years ago, she took the hand Mrs Taylor held out to her, unable to speak.

'Thank you, Ma,' she said, 'It will be lovely for David Joshua to have another Grandma.'

David Joshua turned his head smiled and said 'Grandima.'

Both Mrs Taylor and Val looked at him in amazement, 'That's a new word,' marvelled Val. 'Say that again David Joshua,' she said.

'Grandima,' he shouted with a big giggle as he struggled to get down on the floor. Val let him down and he made straight for Cassie, following her as she ran out of the kitchen to the hall.

'As Jenny and Doug are moving out,' said Val tentatively. 'How would you feel about staying here. Taking over the managing of the house, and David Joshua, while I cope with the next few weeks? We may move to Edwards' farm, but he will be here most days, and I will be happier if I know you are with him.'

'It could get difficult, but we have made the village as safe as we can for what's to come. This would be your home for as long as you wanted, and I will see if I can find someone else to help with the work.' Said Val, fidgeting in her chair, and looking hesitantly at Ma.

'I was wondering how I could help,' said Mrs Taylor with a smile of relief. 'This is perfect for me, come give me a hug, and then do whatever it is you need to do today. He will be fine with me. I know Cassie usually goes with you, but can she stay for now as they have a strong bond, those two?' she commented.

They both got up and Mrs Taylor held Val tight, as Val knew Ma understood how hard it was for her to leave him. Ma having lost a child herself in the past, understood how precious he was. Her child had been about the same age as David Joshua, when he had drowned in the sea, and she had been unable to save him. It had cost Mrs Taylor, her marriage, as her husband had blamed her for her moment of distraction.

Val went to find David Joshua and kissed him goodbye, he wasn't upset at all and turned back to play with Cassie.

'Go' said Mrs Taylor as she ushered Val out of the door, 'they'll both be fine, see you later.'

Val was in a quandary should she find Edward or try and talk to villagers about how they were going to manage to survive. They didn't have much time. Edward won, and she set off to walk the short distance to the farm.

CHAPTER ELEVEN

Arriving at the farm, Val was told by one of his staff that Edward was in the office at the back of the farmhouse. With butterflies in her stomach, she knocked and went in. Edward was sitting at his desk his unruly mop of blond hair a little longer than usual just touching the top of his tee shirt. Tall and muscular the sight of him made her pulse race and realise just how much she loved him, but was he ready to commit to her and David Joshua after all he'd been through?

Edward turned round as he heard Val enter, Val saw a flash of concern on his face before he smiled and said, 'Hi I wasn't expecting you until later, sit down and I'll get you a coffee.' He busied himself making them both a coffee and set it down on the desk as Val closed the door and sat down.

'We have to talk Edward', she said. 'I need to make a decision for all our sakes, especially in the current situation.'

Edward paused for a moment before answering. 'It was such a horrific feeling Val, it felt as if everything I loved was being taken away from me. I could see and understand all that was happening but had no control over it. Derebar (the spirit of Sherebar's dead twin), controlled everything, he caused the accident which allowed him to take over my body but still left a small bit of me conscious. Can you understand the anguish I felt when you seemed to like the new me better than the old, only Cassie and Josh understood something was wrong? When he made love to you, I wanted to give up, but something in me made me want to fight on. I know I couldn't accept David Joshua at first, but it felt as if he wasn't my child, and that him arriving was the ultimate betrayal.'

'I can't promise there won't be problems, but I love you both and want you here with me. Derebar did some good in the fact that he prepared the farm and Village for what's to come, in a way the normal me, couldn't, so we have a better chance of survival. Will you come and live here, I need to know?'

Val stood up and went to him tears running down her cheeks. As he took her in his arms she said. 'I'm sorry I didn't realise something was wrong, I did try a probe to your mind but found it blocked, which I did find strange, but as it's something morally we don't do, I felt guilty at trying, and put it to the back of my mind.'

'It didn't enter my head that something could have invaded your body. It was out of any experience I have ever had. I love you, always have, and if you are willing to talk about it if things get strained, I will move in with David Joshua soon. I've missed you so much, I admit though, it will be difficult to leave my house and I may need to stay there sometimes.'

'Lets' talk about how we do this later,' said Edward still with his arms round Val. He gently kissed her forehead as he wiped her tears. 'Unfortunately, we haven't much time, so we need to make sure the village is organised, or we could all be in trouble. Will you be okay until I can see you later?'

Val nodded her head unable to speak for a moment. Pulling herself together she was conscious that if she didn't hurry, she would be late for her meeting with Mrs Upton and her family. As she went to leave, Edward pulled her to him and kissed her, for a moment it seemed as if they were the only two in the world.

Releasing her Edward said. 'Don't forget I love you; you need to remember that if you start having doubts.' With that he opened the door gave her a little push and closed it behind her. He stood for a minute aware he needed to pull himself together and quell the tiny bit of doubt he felt, when David Joshua looked at him with the intelligent eyes, of someone much older than the child he seemed.

Val was running late, she had to check on her vets' practice before her twelve o'clock meeting. 'How's it all going,' Val asked Hannah as she rushed by.

There's a problem in the lab, I'm just going there,' said a harassed Hannah. 'Can you come with me you may be able to help?'

They went swiftly through the security door into a bright room with work benches full of equipment lining the walls, workstations with computers down the middle, and an area shielded from the main laboratory workspace, by a glass door and large glass wall. Inside there was a space for animal admissions to the operating theatre next door.

A young man was sitting on a chair, head in hands, his body shaking. A woman knelt beside him as she tried to comfort him.

'Hallo Alistair' Hannah said, 'let's get you to the staff room and I'll arrange a drink and you can tell Val and I what's the matter.'

They took him to a small room full of light, with chairs, a table and tea and coffee machine. Val made them all a coffee and they all sat down. *I'm going to get hyper with all this coffee she thought. I wonder how long the stocks of it will last.*

Alistair had stopped shaking but his voice still trembled as he spoke. 'I'm sorry,' he said. 'My wife, daughter and I, love living in this village, but I know more than most what this virus can do, and not being able to talk to anyone outside the Lab is becoming a strain.'

'I'm worried about my Mum, Dad, and Sister. My Dad works on the windfarms but my Mums at home. I don't know if they have been vaccinated or if they will survive. I'm particularly worried about my sister, she's only seventeen. How will she survive if left on her own?'

Val and Hannah looked at each other knowing this was going to be a problem, they couldn't save everyone, but could they knowingly leave a seventeen-year-old girl, to what they knew could happen to her if Thor got hold of her. Her father should have been vaccinated as a key worker, but Val wasn't sure if all wind power sites were on the list.

'I can't promise anything, but I will see what I can do. Write down their details and phone number, we only have eleven days left, after that it will be too late. Go home now and I will update you if I have any news.'

'I'd rather stay here,' said Alistair. 'I know what we are doing is important, and I feel calmer now I've told you. '

'I'll stay for a while Alistair,' said Hannah, 'let's drink our coffee and I'll walk back with you to the lab when you're ready. You go to your meeting Val; we're ok here now.'

Val got up with a sigh, nothing was simple, was it? Especially now. In a way she wished it had already happened, then they would know what they were dealing with, and if they had prepared enough to keep their small corner of the country safe for their children.

She knew they had a better chance than most, because of Sherebar as well as Joe, Jenny, and others with extra abilities and the work already done, but nothing was certain.

CHAPTER TWELVE

She ran all the way to Mrs Upton's house and just arrived in time. The streets were empty, everyone heeding the governments warning to stay at home. At least for the time being.

Mrs Upton opened the door with a big smile and let Val in. The kitchen diner smelt of baking and was full of her family all looking expectantly at Val.

Val realised Mrs Upton had updated them on the situation and it had understandably caused them some consternation.

'Let me start by explaining what we have here, and how you will fit in then I will try and answer any questions', said Val.

'Everyone in this village has been, or will be in the next few days, vaccinated against the Virus. The reason for this was, one, I live here, and with the help of a small group including my family, led by a man called Sherebar, we developed our version of the vaccine. From what we know of the Virus, (*which isn't much* she thought) our version works well.'

'There are small groups around the country that are doing the same, but we can't manufacture enough vaccine to vaccinate the whole country. The vaccine is more complicated than others in the past, and a workable one couldn't be manufactured, even by the government approved labs, in enough quantity to vaccinate everyone in the time available.'

'We had to concentrate our efforts on the survival of those most able to live in the new world after the virus arrives. You won't survive if you are not immune or vaccinated. This village was ideal. It's not too big, but big enough (we hope) to defend itself if needed.'

'It's near the river, the sea and we have two large farms of our own, a Mill, water supply and generate our own electricity. Most houses are on a septic tank type system that works biologically, so we only need a small sewerage system. In the last two years we have been able to attract many of the skills we can use and have built up stocks of materials we may need. Unfortunately, most of the human population of the world will die if their governments haven't organised a vaccination programme in time. Or prepared themselves so that there are enough people around, with the training needed to survive. Those that live may find it hard to survive if they don't have the right skills.' She looked around with interest noting they all seemed to be willing to listen to what she had to say.

'I can answer a few questions now, but don't have long so will do my best in the time I have, otherwise there will be meetings in the next few days. You need to stay indoors as much as you can for now. We don't want to draw attention to ourselves,' said Val. 'I haven't noticed any drones around but that doesn't mean that there isn't an eye in the sky somewhere watching what we do. So be careful.'

'What about accommodation, do we stay where we are

now and what do we do if we need food or clothes?' asked Molly.

'You stay were you are. That will be your home for the near future until we know what the situation is,' said Val. 'Ask your mum and she will arrange food and clothes. Everything will be provided if the requests are reasonable.'

'Mike, if you, Tim, and your families go and meet Jenny at the doctors' she will arrange for you all to be vaccinated today and talk you about how you can help.' continued Val.'

'If any of you teenagers are tech savvy, we can also use your skills. I'll send Josh and Ginny round to explain where teenagers fit in. We need you all to help, including the children, especially at harvest time, we do have teachers, but education will be a bit different from what you are used to. It will also involve survival skills and food production. You may find it more fun than the usual school lessons,' said Val with a wry smile.

'We are asking one from each household to come to a meeting in the village hall tonight, to find out where in the families, we have the skills we need to survive, and how we use them.' Val waited for a moment, while she gathered her thoughts. 'If you can bring a list of skills with you, it would help.' She said.

'It could be gardening, maintenance, teaching, cooking, IT, keep fit, admin. List as many as you can think of. I know this is all frightening, but we have a better chance of surviving together.' She implored them with her eyes for trust, and understanding, knowing this must be frightening for them, but unity was essential.

'How is it you have the right to tell us what to do?' challenged the eldest of the boys.

'For the moment my team, and myself will run the village,' said Val. 'Because we have the knowledge to do it. If you don't help you don't eat or deserve to be here. I know it's hard to understand what it's going to be like, but to be blunt at least half the population will die, perhaps many more.'

The boy hung his head and shuffled his feet, his face red with embarrassment.

Val saw this, and realised she needed to soften her voice. She didn't want to alienate them too much but wanted the teenagers to understand this was serious. 'You are young and the future, but you need to help me make sure you have one. It could be exciting or dangerous, we just don't know. Talk to Josh and Ginny, they are teens too, and fun to be with. You may find you like being here after all.'

Continuing with more confidence now she had their undivided attention, Val continued. 'Once we know what we are dealing with, I promise we will set up a Village council including all villagers over fourteen to discuss any future. Is that, Ok?' Val queried.

The boy nodded, a bit shocked at the answer, but seemingly willing to reserve judgment until meeting Josh and Ginny.

'So sorry but I have to go now, there is so much still to do,' she said pausing to take in a deep breath. As she opened the door to leave, Josh and Ginny came round the corner. 'Hi, you two, have you come to show these three around? Don't forget to stay indoors as much as possible.' She had to grin to herself as she wondered what the newcomers would think of them both.

Billy and the others gazed in amazement at the pair before them. Ginny in her jagged rainbow top, bright orange pants and big boots. Josh, Strong, confident with a mop of hair covering his intelligent eyes. Both knowing exactly what this three were thinking.

'Come on, get your coats and we will show you where the fun is going to start,' said Josh. We need to get under cover soon and show you where you should be when the alarm goes.'

Val turned and watched as the small group trouped towards the baker's shop.

Got their priorities sorted she thought with a smile as she hurried along.

CHAPTER THIRTEEN

Val, and her group all met at Edwards Farm before the evening meeting.

'Josh was annoyed he wasn't asked to be here,' said Hannah. 'He said he was as involved as anyone, he's cross that no one has realised how strong Ginny is either.'

'He's right,' said Jenny, 'he's been through a lot with us the past two years.' Although Hannah didn't know just how involved he'd been, as she wasn't aware of all his hidden abilities. Jenny smiled as she continued. 'If he comes, Ginny will have to come too, they've become inseparable in the brief time they've known each other, and we don't know much about her yet.'

'Why don't we ask them to our next get together and bring them to tonight's meeting. We need all the teenagers to come. They're going to have to help more than they expect, and we need to make sure they all understand why.'

'What do we do about Alistair's family? asked Val. 'We could use his dad here managing the energy plant, but how do we get them here?' Time is getting short for us to do anything.'

'I'll speak to him tomorrow,' said Edward. 'Have we still got room to house them.'

'We have a small cottage they could use,' said Hannah but that's the last space we have. We need to keep some for the children we might have to take in.'

'We better get going,' said Jenny. 'We have some organising to do and plans to make.'

The village meeting was a bustling success, but managing their food supply was a hot topic, but a group of villagers that could work together was formed, agreeing that all food would be put in the central market, and provision made to store and preserve a portion for the winter.

The villagers spoke about the fact that there may be other survivors around that needed helping. Security would be paramount, explained Edward, and stores for the future would be kept by the farm's underground facilities.

Although Edward was uncomfortable about it, it was another provision Dererbar had made, to make sure they survived to look after David Joshua. Everyone would be needed at harvest time even though they had working robots. It would be hard, but it would mean they would live.

Hannah confirmed that several farming families nearby had been vaccinated, so that may help the food situation too once they were able to contact them.

Edward went home to phone Alistair's family, leaving Val and the others to finish.

Alistair was waiting at the door. 'I thought I ought to be here,' he said,' 'I think my family should come tomorrow, don't you? Security may get tighter in the next few days. I'll feel much happier when they're here.'

'Okay,' agreed Edward, 'come in,' and took Alistair to his office. 'This is a secure phone, your conversation will be scrambled, but your Dads won't, so tell him to just answer yes or no. I need to speak to him at the end of your conversation.' With that he passed Alistair the phone.

'Dad' said Alistair as his father answered the phone. 'Don't talk just listen and then answer yes or no. Don't say my name. Have you, Mum or Ella been vaccinated recently?

'No' said his Dad,

'A virus is on the debris of the meteor that is going to hit us in a few days' time. If you are not vaccinated, you will not survive. It's what I have been working on. I thought you would be classed as a key worker, and all of you vaccinated so wasn't too worried. That was until I saw your site wasn't on the secret Government document, that my boss had somehow acquired from her brother. You need to leave tonight; I can't explain more, please come. You can help us here. Will you come?' pleaded Alistair.

After a pause, his dad said, 'yes.' Alistair handed the phone to Edward.

'I am sending an app to your phone. If you have a problem don't hesitate to press it, and we'll be able to find you, even if your phone is taken by those wishing to stop you. It will disappear from your phone as soon as it's pressed. Bring as much equipment as possible but don't worry about anything else,' said Edward.

'Leave as it's getting dark tomorrow; I'll send instructions on your phone. This will disappear if you are stopped. We will find you if that happens but hope it won't come to that. Do you understand?'

'Yes', agreed Alistair's dad. Edward cut the call.

'Will they make it out safely?" asked Alistair.

'I hope so,' said Edward, 'but Thor's active in that vicinity, and your dad would be valuable to them. They have a stash of vaccine to use as bribes for those they want working for them.'

'Why haven't the government commandeered it?' queried Alistair. 'Surely, they have the power?'

'They tried and were partially successful, Val's brother Joe was able to hack Thor's system for a while and divert deliveries to the government vaccination facility. The vaccine is now well hidden, they've made sure of that, and it's being sold to the highest bidder. Their one doesn't work as well as ours in tests, and they don't have large stores of it.'

Edward shrugged his shoulders and ran his fingers through his hair in frustration, as he continued.

'Thor are clever, and run ultimately by those of Sherebar's race, who are not concerned about the survival of humans, unless they are useful to them. The involvement by this race, gives Thor extra power to outwit the Government, and they won't hesitate to use it. These beings think they should rule the world unlike Sherebar's group who want to help it.

CHAPTER FOURTEEN

Alistair's dad, went to his workshop the next morning to load a van with parts, manuals, and anything else he thought may be useful. It worked in his favour that there was only a skeleton staff, due to most staff staying at home, no one questioned why one of the chief engineers was loading one of the larger vans, as they were all doing extra jobs now. It was agony not being able to warn his staff, but he didn't know what good it would do, as he wasn't able to obtain any vaccination for them.

He wouldn't know if there was any way to help them, until he saw Alistair and talked to him about it. He busied himself all day but was very worried about a young lad with no family working for him, who was a promising engineer. He made a quick decision as he was leaving to take him with them.

'Lewis,' he called to the young lad. 'Here a minute, have you anything on tonight? I need you with me to check an installation up North, be away a couple of days. We need to leave now.'

'I'll have to pick up a few clothes,' said Lewis as he agreed. Looking happy to get out of the workshop for a while.

They stopped at Lewis's flat as he packed a holdall, and then drove to Georges' house where George's wife Helen and daughter Ella were waiting. Lewis looked questioningly at George. Who said, 'I'm taking them with me for a break didn't want to leave them alone with this lockdown looming. Can you sit in the back, there's a pull-down seat just there?' Pointing at a space behind the front seats.

As Ella and Helen got into the front of the van and Lewis climbed over to sit in the back, George said. 'Lewis is coming with us to help me.' Ella was sulking as she didn't want to go, and Helen wondered why George insisted they came, but sensed there was something more to this that he didn't want to discuss. So knowing him well, didn't query it.

They had travelled for two hours, and the sun was dipping below the horizon and the sky turning an inky blue, when a car raced by and turned across the road making it impossible to pass. Looking in the mirror George saw another blocking the road behind. He quickly realised they were in trouble. He pressed the app on this phone which immediately sent out a distress signal and said to Lewis. 'Take the phone and hide it, whatever happens.'

'Hide in the back now, and don't make a sound,' he said to Lewis. 'If they don't discover you, get out later and hide. Don't go for help, it will be on its way, and they will find you.' 'Who?' asked Lewis, his voice trembling, but George didn't have time to answer.

A man all in black carrying a gun walked towards them, pulled a screaming Ella out of the van, and said curtly to George. 'Follow me and she won't be hurt. Try to escape and she's dead.'

To Ella he said,' 'shut up or I'll shut you up. If your Dad behaves, you'll all be okay.' With that he pushed her in the waiting car and got in beside her. Ella quietened, clearly terrified of what was going to happen next. George had no choice but to comply, but he glanced back at the van, and prayed that Lewis stayed hidden.

~

On his farm Edward received the SOS call he had dreaded. He alerted Jenny, Doug, and Val. They met in the secure room at the farm and dialled Joe, Sally, and Sherebar. A large screen descended from the wall and a picture of a dilapidated farm appeared with George's van outside. As they watched, the back of the van slowly opened, and a young man got out.

'He's got Georges' phone,' said Edward as they watched him quietly run to the bushes and hide. 'Can you contact him Joe, and tell him to get as far away as possible, George must have bought him with them? Val's indicating he's not a threat.'

Joe, Sally, and Sherebar appeared on another screen. Joe gave a thumbs up indicating Lewis had answered the phone's vibration. Joe had dimmed the screen so that it didn't give Lewis's position away.

'Help is on its way, but you must get as far away from here as possible,' said Joe to Lewis.

'We will pick you up once we have rescued the others. Can you quickly tell us what happened?'

Lewis explained the situation, and said he wanted to stay and help, but Joe told him he needed to get out of there now, he would be a hindrance. It was urgent he did as he was told.

They watched as Lewis moved off over the fields, Joe tracking the signal as he went.

'Can you deactivate the phone but still track him,' asked

Doug. 'As I'm worried it's Thor and they will pick up the activity and send someone to investigate.'

'Yes', said Joe, 'It's all-in hand. We can update you on the farm layout, where they are held, and Sally and I can give Doug and Edward a bit of protection, but otherwise you're on your own.'

Sherebar interrupted, 'They want Alistair, and will use his family to get to him. I should have realised he was vulnerable. You need to make sure he doesn't leave. They'll kill them all anyway, once they have what they want.'

'How do we do that?' asked Jenny, 'we can't lock him up.'

'Tell him the truth' said Sherebar. 'It's vital he does as you ask and stay in the village. He's more likely to do that, if you're honest with him, explain your rescue mission, make him realise he would be a hinderance, and not any help. You must leave now, there's little time to spare. Take the dart guns Jenny, Val, watch how you guard your minds, there may be someone there who is able to invade them,' continued Sherebar.

CHAPTER FIFTEEN

At Josh's' home Josh silently crept to Ginny's' room and gently shook her awake, a finger to his lips to warn her to be quiet.

'Somethings going on' he whispered. If you want to come with me, get dressed in black and I'll wait downstairs, be quiet as we don't want to wake Mum and David.'

Ginny met him in the kitchen, and they crept outside.

'What's happening?' queried Ginny.

'I'm not sure, as Val and Jenny block their minds, but it must be serious as there is a lot of brain noise, it woke me up, I'm just picking up Dooley and my Bow and dart guns then we will try and find out.' He gave a low whistle and Dooley his rat companion in other adventures, jumped into his pocket. He unlocked the outhouse, took out a small bow and a sheath full of arrows and the hidden guns.

Josh and Ginny made their way as silently as they could, to the garage where the special car was kept. It was large, silent, didn't need lights in the dark and was bullet proof. Hiding in the dark, as they heard Val, Jenny, Edward, and Doug arrive deep in conversation.

'I think one of us should stay behind,' said Doug. 'This is going to be chancy, and someone needs to be able to run the installations.'

'Sherebar would send someone,' answered Jenny. 'We work better together.'

'We also have two more to add to the mix,' added Val. 'Come out you two, I can feel you hiding in the corner.'

'We're coming,' said Josh forcefully. 'Together Ginny and I are as strong as you.'

'He's right,' agreed Edward. 'Remember, I've seen him in action and that was months ago now. He saved my life.'

'Get in then,' said Val crossly with a shrug of resignation. 'We don't have time for arguments, no acting on your own like last time Josh, it's dangerous.'

It took them an hour to get near the disused farm, Doug and Edward had tiny ear communicators on, so that they could hear Joe's directions as they couldn't connect with their mind as well as the others.

They all silently left the car and made their way towards the buildings, Joe had prewarned them that there were four men outside and two inside.

They decided that Jenny and Val would take on the two men at the front, Josh, and Ginny one at the back and Doug the one at the side while Edward would investigate entry to the building.

The two men were talking when they heard a noise. 'Come out or I shoot, we have you covered,' said one drawing his gun.

They were amazed when a woman in a short skirt and long dark hair came tottering through the bushes carrying a bottle of what looked like Gin.

'Civilisation at last,' she cried waving the bottle around, taking no notice of the gun. 'Are you one of those adventure stags' parties, can I join in?'

For a moment, the men were overwhelmed with the sexual alure emanating from the woman, but just as they came to their senses they were hit in the chest with such pain, they both fell to the ground unconscious and the apparition of the woman disappeared.

Jenny and Val looked at each other and smiled. 'We haven't lost it then,' whispered Jenny alluding to the power they had just used so effectively.

'We may need to help Doug.' Said Val.

'What about Josh and Ginny?' queried Jenny.

'Don't worry about them,' answered Val. 'As they said, together they're stronger than us, they just need learn how to use their powers properly. They have to practice as they may have to depend on those powers in the future.'

Josh and Ginny had located the fourth man and Dooley had called on the many rats at the dilapidated farm to help.

The man gave a yelp as sharp teeth bit into his ankle, as he spun round trying to shake the rats off, Josh took aim with his bow, and the arrow found its mark anesthetising the man for several hours.

Josh said. 'Dooley, can you and your friends check under Mr Greens van for a tracker and destroy it while we decide what to do next? You may want to make a meal of the gang's car tyres too.'

Suddenly Ginny stopped and listened, 'The girls in trouble,' she said softly, 'let's see if we can get in.'

They crept round the back to where a dim light was shining through a gap in a dirty curtain. A man had a young girl by the arm and laughing while she tried to get away, his gun trained on her mother who was tied to a chair.

'You'll all be dead by the end of tomorrow,' he said to Alistair's Mum. 'Even when we get your son, but I may keep you,' he smirked at the girl.

'We've got to get in there quickly,' said Ginny getting agitated.

They tried to open the side door, but it was locked. Ginny took a pin from her hair, and it was soon opened.

A girl of many talents thought Josh as they silently crept along the corridor to the room Helen and Ella were being kept by their captors. Outside the door Ginny focused her energy on the gun.

The man holding it looked puzzled for a moment then dropped the gun with a cry as it got hotter and hotter until it was burning his hand. Ella pulled away from him and ran to untie her mother as Josh and Ginny exploded into the room, Ginny picking up the gun and aiming it at the man.

The man trying to make sense of what just happened, lunged at Ginny.

'Keep away or I'll shoot,' she said.

'I don't think so honey,' he said menacingly. 'Give me the gun.'

Ginny looked at him with utter disgust and shot him in the leg.

'I do what I say,' she said as he rolled around in agony.

'Ella, help your mum,' said Josh, 'the keys to your van are on the table outside. Can you drive it, do you feel well enough? He asked Helen, 'You need to get out of here before others arrive.'

'Yes,' nodded Helen shakily her face grey with worry, 'but I don't know where to go, and what about my husband, I heard screaming?'

'He'll be with you soon. The others will bring him,' said Josh with more confidence than he felt. There was a large amount of pain in the air, and he wasn't sure who's it was.

'I'll go with you.' said Ginny to Helen and Ella. 'Josh, can you put him out of his misery, the noise is getting on my nerves?' Pointing to the man on the floor.

'Joe's saying there is someone called Lewis to pick up on the way Ginny, he'll tell you when to stop,' said Josh. As he concentrated on the man rolling around the floor. He stilled his mind then tied him up securely on the chair Helen had vacated.

Ella and Helen didn't understand what was happening but followed Ginny out into the dim hall, she picked up the van keys and ran to the van keeping as quiet as possible. They heard a scream come from the farm and hesitated, but Ginny put her hand to her lips to shush them and urged them on.

That was sloppy, thought Ginny as she jumped in the van, *leaving keys around like that.*

Josh crept along the corridor towards the noise and saw Edward outside a door. Looking through the window in the door, Edward saw George with blood pouring from his nose, and what looked like a wound on his head. He was slumped forward only the ropes keeping him in place.

Edward was so angry his kicked open the door, dart gun raised, and fired at the man as he entered. This didn't have any effect on the kidnapper at all, who fired back at Edward, hitting him in the chest. This also wasn't effective as Edward was wearing one of the special protective suits Joe had sent.

'Well, well,' said the captor with a smile. 'Stalemate I think, although I have the advantage of powers you don't have. You've learnt to block your mind I see, but don't have any of my power there.'

'But I do,' said Josh as he launched himself through the

open door, firing, his arrow, and sending a powerful blast into the captor's mind.

The abductor swayed but regained his balance, just as Val and Jenny arrived having received Josh's cries for help.

Together the three of them sent an instant beam that incapacitated the abductors body, wiped his mind, and he slowly sank to the floor.

Edward untied George, whose wrists were bleeding and his face badly bruised. As he was now unconscious and unable to walk, Edward gently eased him over his shoulders, as Jenny said. 'We must get going, he was strong, (pointing at the man on the floor), and won't be out long. Doug's at the car.'

'What happened to Doug's one?' asked Josh, as they made their way slowly to the car due to George's condition.

'He thought he saw a snake in the grass, and as he was distracted Doug sent him to sleep with a dart,' grinned Jenny.

'I didn't think Doug could project like that,' laughed Josh lightening the atmosphere.

'He can't,' smiled Jenny, 'the stupid man sat on a log for a smoke and put his foot on an adder nest. Thor really should be more careful who they choose to do their dirty jobs. Although the main abductor was a bit of a surprise, we'll have to be aware of that possibility in the future.'

They carefully laid George in the back of the car and covered him with a blanket. 'Can you sit with him Val?' asked Doug. 'Tell me if there is any change, he's in a bad way, I'll need to take him straight to the surgery he may need his head stitched.'

The car silently glided over the roads arriving outside the surgery and small vet practise theatre without incident. Dr Foster and a nurse were waiting and carefully loaded George onto a trolley, took him inside and cleaned him up while Doug got ready to treat him.

Jenny, Josh, and Edward went to find food while they waited for Doug. The kitchen was warm there was a pot of something good smelling and comforting, in the oven. Ma's been here thought Jenny. She really was like an adoptive mother to them all. Just what you needed in a crisis,

When they had finished eating, Val and Josh went looking for Ginny, Ella, Lewis, and Helen, at Josh's farm.

Hannah gave a big sigh of relief when she saw Ginny, only realising they'd gone when Bel came into her room, saying Ginny wasn't in her bed. When Ginny turned up, she knew Josh wouldn't be far away. She didn't ask questions, she understood from experience they wouldn't be answered, having an inkling of how special Josh, Ginny, and the others were.

She had made them all soup and crusty bread and had managed to persuade Helen and Ella to eat something. Ginny and Lewis hadn't lost their appetite and were ladling more soup into their bowls.

'How is my husband?' Helen asked Val, her voice trembling. 'Did you rescue him, where is he? Can I see him? Where's Alistair?'

'He's going to be okay,' Val soothed, 'Doug's treating him now and will give your husband something to make him comfortable and sleep. It's best he stays in the surgery recovery room for the night. You can visit with him, but it would be better for you to be with Ella and Lewis and get a good night's sleep if you can. I promise to let you know if there's a problem.'

'Was Dad savagely beaten?' asked Ella. 'We heard the screams and couldn't help. It was so scary.' Her voice wobbled, and she angrily brushed tears from her eyes.

'He was beaten and needs stitches,' admitted Val. 'but

mostly he needs sleep. He knows you're safe, so he's got less to worry about. Let's find your brother and let him know you are well. We told him you were with us. I've arranged for you all to stay near him.'

The next few days went swiftly as there was so much to organise, George slowly improved with Helen and Alistair at his side. Ginny and Josh introduced Ella and Lewis to the others in the teenage group they had formed, and they realised Ella's technical skills would be of help to them. She also had a good understanding of engineering principles, learnt from her dad.

The atmosphere was becoming tense as the day of impact drew near. The information room in the village had screens following the meteors progress.

They knew attempts to divert the expected Asteroid and meteor air burst had failed. Some of the teenagers though it was like living in one of their games and was quite fun, not realising that they couldn't just resurrect themselves when the game ended. This was real life from now on.

CHAPTER SIXTEEN

Sherebar sent Val the signal she had been dreading, it woke her up. She thought she had been prepared but found she was shaking, felt sick, her hands were clammy, and for a minute she didn't know what to do. Then the adrenalin kicked in and she shook Edward awake. 'It's happening' she said 'Hurry we must warn everyone to stay indoors. Jenny and Dough are meeting us in the control room.'

She watched as it took him a minute to understand what was happening. Val was already dressed, and Edward threw on some clothes. Val called to Ma to watch David Joshua, and they both ran to the control room down the corridor.

Dough and Jenny had already let themselves in and Josh and Ginny were not far behind carrying bags of burgers and fries.

'Told mum we would be hungry, so she sent these', said Josh with a grin.

'Might have known you two wouldn't be far away', said Val with exasperation.

'This is serious, you are not to go outside now, do you both understand?

'Yes,' said Ginny, 'we do, and we aren't stupid Val. We don't need protecting. Josh and I want to see what we are up against as much as you do. 'Look' she pointed, as she reached for a burger from the bag she was carrying and took a bite, Hannah's tomato sauce dripping down her chin. 'It's started.'

They all crowded round the screen. Joe had made sure all their equipment would work. Having the benefit of Sherebar's advanced technology, and being able to use the natural radio waves of the universe in ways not seen before, was an advantage.

They watched in silence at the amazing light show in the sky that enticed so many to ignore warnings to stay inside.

'Can we make sure the warnings to the villagers to stay indoors, is broadcast every fifteen minutes?' asked Doug.

'Josh and I talked to our friends and warned them in very graphic terms what would happen to them. We showed them a video Josh made with lots of dead bodies lying around to get the message through.' said Ginny her eyes still glued to the screen.

'You what!' said Jenny agitatedly. 'We don't want to scare them to death.'

'Haven't you seen the games we all play? What I showed them wouldn't frighten a child,' said Josh.

'Oh no' said Val softly, as the picture showed a London Street. People were falling, coughing up a greenish liquid, then lying still. A man still standing shouted get indoors, as he grabbed the hand of a small child.

The pictures changed New York, Sydney, Nairobi, Cape town, Mosco, Beijing all showing similar views. The virus was acting swiftly. The wind was helping to spread it throughout the world.

A message came from Sherebar, some Aboriginal people,

Māori's, those with true Cornish blood and some African tribes, seemed to have immunity. There may be more, he said.

How many others, and why Cornwall? Val asked, not really expecting answer.

They watched for hours until they were so exhausted, eyes drooping, they were finding it hard to stay awake, Doug suggested they'd seen enough and needed sleep. 'We'll be no good to anyone if we are all tired,' he said.

'You two need to stay here tonight, no sneaking off, it's still too dangerous to go out. There's a room with bunk beds next door. I'll let Hannah know,' said Val to Ginny and Josh. 'Please do as you are told you two, just this once. I don't want to have to worry about you all night as well, it may seem as if I'm moaning a lot, but I love you and want you to be safe.'

Despite the seriousness of the situation, Ginny's eyes filled with tears at her words. Val guessed that having someone care for her like that, was probably a new experience.

CHAPTER SEVENTEEN

Morning dawned and reality took hold. Mrs Taylor had made sure breakfast was ready as she felt the despair in the air. The day ahead would be hard, and so she took David Joshua, Cassie, and Buster to the playroom for games, as no one was allowed out. All doors were locked. Buster and Cassie were subdued as they felt the heaviness of the atmosphere. They lay under the table and even Buster couldn't be coaxed out by food.

The village communication system warned that it could mean death if anyone ventured out. Although all the village had been vaccinated, it was an extra safety precaution. The all clear would be broadcast by the village loudspeaker when Dr Foster and Doug felt it would be safe. This time it seemed, everyone took note, no one ventured out.

The village was as quiet as death itself. A dark shadow hung over the world.

In rooms all over the world, populations were waking up to a new reality. Probably not ready to cope with what lay ahead.

Ginny and Josh were first into the breakfast room, their stomachs rumbling hungry as usual.

'I need to check if Bel and Tip are oaky,' said Ginny anxiously to Josh, as she helped herself to a plate of bacon and eggs.

'We can do that from the screen in the control room,' said Josh gently. 'Also, Mum has text that they are all fine, but Bel and Tip may like to speak to you for some reassurance.'

The others arrived, but everyone was subdued, no one felt much like talking. So they ate in silence then took their drinks with them into the control room.

They tuned in to Joe and Sherebar, and a haggard Joe came on screen.

'Are you ready for this?' Joe queried, 'it's pretty bad '.

Doug looked round the room. 'Are you two okay with this?' he asked Ginny and Josh. 'If not, it's not anything to be ashamed off.'

'It can't be as bad as some of the things I've seen, Doug,' claimed Ginny. 'I'm staying.'

'So am I,' agreed Josh. 'We have to know what we are dealing with, without any whitewash.'

'Okay' said Joe. 'The areas in grey are where we think Thor is active.'

A map of the world came up on the screen, focusing on Paris.

A row of large lorries with people in hazard suits, were picking up bodies lying in the street and putting them in the lorries. Everything was silent, no movement in the houses. So many bodies, and possibly hundreds more in the surrounding tenement flats.

One of the figures stopped as if listening then ran into one of the buildings and after a few minutes came out with a crying bundle in a blanket. Others stopped to look, as the bundle, a small child, was put in the cab. Once the lorries were full, they trundled off with their terrible load to feed the fires now burning all over the country.

In both Italy and Spain, the story was the same. There were grey areas in the Basque Country. Florida, South America, Brazil, Africa. Some bigger than others.

'Is this where Thor is located?' Doug asked Joe with concern, indicating the grey areas. Having had unpleasant contact with them in the past.

'Yes,' agreed Joe.

One of screens suddenly went blank and then Sherebar appeared on this, and then stepped out into the room.

'Wow! How did you do that?' asked Josh in admiration.

'I'll show you one day, but for now you can understand how bad it's going to be. Disposal of so many bodies will be difficult, as most will need to be buried. Parks and fields are being dug up as crematoriums can't cope.' Said Sherebar. 'It will take at least two years or more to clear the houses and streets, but our pressing problem will be containing Thor. They caused us problems when we were making the vaccine and they won't stop now.'

'What about here?' queried Doug.

'Many have died,' confirmed Sherebar, 'but the government here didn't sell vaccines to the highest bidder. They went first to those needed to keep a semblance of health, order, and security, as well as their own families as expected. Although it was a challenging thing to do, it will be shown to be the right way, given the limited amount of vaccine we could produce. This Country is in a better place to survive than most. If Thor can be defeated.'

With an ironic smile Sherebar continued. 'Even Thor did not vaccinate violent criminals, or drug lords, or they did, it wasn't the vaccine the criminals thought they were buying, but a fake no good to stop any virus. They were vaccinating those they would need for their workforce, and security.

Those most useful to them.' He smiled at them, but it was a smile of sadness and regret at the way of life lost. He continued.

'Thor made sure any elements of the criminal society more powerful than them did not survive. World domination is what they want, and powerful beings of my race are in charge. Not the idiots you see doing their dirty work.'

'There will be children with no families, who will need teaching practical skills to survive. Marika who you met, has set up homes already, but we will need more. Can you make room here?' '

Jenny was the first to speak. 'We'll do what we can. We have limited accommodation ready, but we will need more teachers unless our teenagers can help.'

'I'll speak to you in more detail when we have all the figures,' said Sherebar.as he disappeared abruptly from the room. 'I have to go now,'

Joe said,' I must go too, there is work to do keeping communication open, but I will keep in touch.' With a quick wave he also left.

As all of them in the control room were weary, the night, and what they had seen taking its toll. They decided to take a break and make plans later. Ginny and Josh found a quiet room and spent the next few hours trying to make contact around the world. The wall of silence was deafening.

'There must be someone out there somewhere Josh,' cried Ginny. Realising for the first time just how terrible this virus was, and how lucky she was to be alive.

CHAPTER EIGHTEEN

Two Years Later.

The last two years had been hard for the survivors, finding food, coping with grief, and physically challenging, without the services most of the population had used unthinkingly. Post was intermittent, rubbish collection, and supermarkets non-existent. Most hadn't realised the extent of the devastation that would be caused.

Many people had survived the virus in Britain. thanks to the vaccination program, but millions had died. Too many to bury or cremate. Leaving large cities to the ghosts of the dead.

The bodies had decomposed, and the smell had gone, Cities, towns and villages decimated, now quiet, and with no soul without the hustle and bustle of everyday life, there was no longer a housing crisis, as there were so many empty properties. The virus didn't make you ill, if you weren't immune or vaccinated it killed you, rich or poor it didn't discriminate.

Small communities were surviving, but in a vastly different world. Nature was taking back control. The World was greener, and there had even been rain in the desert bringing colour and a vibrancy that hadn't been seen for centuries. Animals weren't effected by the virus. Nature was healing the natural world, bringing hope amid the carnage?

Food hadn't been too much of a problem yet as there was plenty to be scavenged, but it was now being rationed where the Government had control. There were no significant imports with large boats and planes out of action and people scarce on farms, and manufacturing from abroad non-existent. Farms and food suppliers locally were going to need to be prioritised. How many of these had survived was still not known.

Communications were possible, but difficult, and fuel scarce. Luckily most vehicles were electric or solar powered now. The electric supply had been protected by those in a secretive government department, who realised the importance to the regeneration of the country. The depleted Government were finding it a struggle to keep control of the population that was left. The Army was helping for the moment, but how long this would last was a worry for the surviving government. Their loyalty was to the King who had survived and was proving his worth by joining with the troops in their efforts to bring a semblance of order in the chaos.

No one was getting paid due to the government's inability to collect tax, however there was plenty to salvage. How long that would be the case was open to speculation within the Government.

Some countries had fared better than others, but all had lost a large part of their populations. Would they be able to trade with each other? Had enough sailors, drivers, and pilots survived. Was there still the energy available to fuel the transport in already underdeveloped countries? Many unanswerable questions facing the Government.

At the farm Ginny looked out of the window. The farmyard was busy, and Bel and Tip were much happier here. They had settled well. This life was better in every way to the one they'd left behind, and Hannah and Edward's Dad had taken the place of a mum and dad they would have loved, but never had. Ginny sometimes yearned for the freedoms of the old world. Were you could at least dream of going to the cinema, a party, and travel the world.

She knew she would have made something of her life or was that just a dream? Giving herself a mental shake, she picked up her jacket and went to meet Josh. The world was so different now. They hadn't felt the whole horror here but had witnessed it on their screens and were aware of the carnage imposed on the world. Josh as usual, was his old cheerful self and that did her head in sometimes.

Josh was in the control room with Ella, Lewis, Val, Edward, Jenny, and Doug.

'Hi Ginny,' welcomed Val with a warm smile. 'There's Hot chocolate from Hannah's secret store and croissants from the bakery, I thought we'd treat ourselves as we have some difficult discissions to make'.

'We thought we would share the updates from Sherebar and decide where we go forward. There's a group called the Scavengers that are finding anything that can be reused, and in some cases eaten. They have taken over empty houses and buildings as storehouses for the goods they find. Unfortunately, Thor is still operational, and there are rumours that they are kidnapping adults and children, to work on their farms and factories. A few farms are still growing food, but distribution is a problem. Although there are electric lorries available when drivers are trained by the army.'

'Can we see the evidence Sherebar sent,' asked Josh. 'Do we know what the rest of the world is like?'

With a sigh, Val pushed a button, and a large screen descended. Looking as if they had been taken from a drone or plane, images appeared.

Sherebar still had the ability to do this then, Ginny thought.

The first showed the whole of the UK. A voiceover explained the red dots were areas that were inhabited. Then it slowly panned over the rest of the world. Smaller countries (for example Sweden, Denmark, Finland, Ireland) seemed to have managed to vaccinate 30% of their population, whereas India, Pakistan, China, Russia, and America had large areas without habitation. The larger the area the worse it became.

There had been no official communication with China or Russia although information from small groups on the ground had filtered through to intelligence in Britain.

'Does Thor have access to this?' said Josh worriedly. 'It would be easy for it to pick off areas around the world if it does.'

'No, Thor doesn't, but this must be kept so secret that this broadcast will be destroyed, now we have viewed it,' answered Val.

'What use is it to us?' queried Ginny. 'Doesn't Thor have access to the same drones or satellites to give the identical information?'

'Not now, but it won't be long before Thor has that capability. Sherebar's people were better prepared, and his access and knowledge of the workings of the world are superior,' said Val with a sigh, her body sagging a bit with the weight of this knowledge.

'It also shows us the extent of Thor's facility in Colchester,' confirmed Val, zooming into the area. 'We may start seeing them flexing their muscles soon, it also gives us an idea of where some survivors are being held.' She ran a hand over her face trying to dispel the tiredness she felt before continuing. 'Sherebar will be sending us more detailed information on our area, I don't think the reformed Government will be sending anyone our way just yet. They have other things to deal with, but we won't let anyone commandeer our people or resources without a fight. We may have to vaccinate again and need to keep our research facility running.' Val continued, her voice wavering with a tremor, showing her concern.

'Also, according to Sherebar there have been no births which were not conceived before the virus anywhere in the World in the last two years. No one knows if this is temporary, or how it will affect what happens in the future. I don't know, either, what that means for the survival humankind. Or how Sherebar knows that. Or if it has anything to do with the virus. Or if Thor had a hand in this anomaly.' Taking a breath Val paused, as she looked around at the concerned faces of those present.

'Shouldn't we be looking to see if we can help anyone nearby?' Interrupted Josh.

'Yes,' agreed Val. 'but we need to keep up our defences, training the youngsters how best to keep themselves safe, and to make sure our food stocks are secure. Let's discuss the areas we can concentrate on first. Our farms and orchards are productive and the robots are still working, which is a bonus, so we have food. Not the variety we had before, but not bad.' Indicating Edward, she said. 'Edward has been careful to preserve any surplus, but glass containers could become a problem, and any we find, need to be stored for re-use. What about health issues Doug?' asked Val

'Medical stores are acceptable, but I need to take a visit to the abandoned hospital outside the village, to save as many more medicines as possible. There's a lot of good equipment there, and if we can find the vaccinated staff, I may be able to open a small part of the hospital in the future.' Continued Doug his face grim, as he contemplated the future. 'I'm going to try and contact my partners in my old practice. What about farm equipment and services Edward? Do you have an update?'

'We supply all our own services and George oversees any repairs. We're lucky to have him. He's completely recovered from his injuries. We've been able to source materials and parts from abandoned warehouses, but George and I are aware that won't last forever. Something we need to think about,' said Edward with a serious expression.

'How are the teenagers coping,' Jenny asked Josh and Ginny who had been quiet up to now. Unusual for them.

'They've been occupied helping on the farm and learning survival skills, but couldn't we have some fun too. A cinema night, football, music,' answered Josh.

'Josh and I can amuse ourselves,' said Ginny. 'We have access to Joe and superior technology, and we have been teaching self-defence but, if you don't want unhappy teenagers, some more variety would be good.'

'I'll think about it. I could devise some new games for our system so they could have some fun time online too,' said Jenny thoughtfully.

'I have to get back to work,' said Edward, 'can we continue this later?'

They all agreed there was a lot to think about. *All we can do is our best,* thought Val as the meeting broke up.

Jenny was going to show Val a programme that she had just developed, so she stayed behind. It was a chance for them to be together on their own for a change.

Josh and Ginny disappeared. Doug watched them go with a smile. 'They certainly livened up the place.' He said to Val as he got up to go. 'I must go back to the surgery; normal problems don't go away, just because there has been a pandemic.' Bye Jenny, I'll see you later.' He said blowing her a kiss. With that he disappeared too.

CHAPTER NINETEEN

Ginny was bored and fed up with being told what her and Josh, could and couldn't do. The countryside was there to be explored. They wanted to find if there was anything they could use around before other scavengers found it. Val had said that many farm families had been vaccinated, so there must be life near. Ginny wondered why they hadn't been contacted.

'Let's take the van, it's fully charged,' said Josh understanding her mood. 'They won't miss us if we block our minds.'

'Where's the key?' asked Ginny, without a thought of the consequences.

'Hanging in the farm office. Mums at Val's clinic. Come on let's see if we can find them.'

Josh, being bought up on a farm could drive most things, and Ginny had learned to drive at the farm in the last year. Access to vehicles was limited but most were topped up and ready to go, just in case of an emergency.

Ginny knew they'd be in trouble if they were caught, but

decided they needed a bit of excitement in life just now, so she was prepared to risk it.

Soon they were on the road. The fields rolled by the sun shone, and there was no one around. *Freedom,* thought Ginny, grinning at Josh, and singing at the top of her voice. Josh soon joined in, and it felt good to be young and on an adventure for a change. Most in the village had stayed in walking distance of home in the past two years, understandably trying to survive, their priority.

Ginny and Josh decided to aim for the next village which was about twenty miles away. It was wonderful to be out. The sun on her skin, and a breeze in her hair with Josh by her side. A good friend like no other, who made her feel alive and happy. Fields rolled by everything was green and the birds were in full voice, they saw a hare hiding in the hedgerow and a fox lazily surveying the fields for prey, his eyes glinting in the sunlight.

Eventually they came to the village, and it was a bit of a jolt to find everything deserted and eerily quiet. They stopped for a minute to take in the reality of what had happened, and even though they expected it, it was a bit of a shock to find everything abandoned. It really was a ghost town. There was no one around, the properties empty with gardens overgrown, and the whole place had no soul. Only the ghosts of those who had once bought life and bustle to the Village. It was a bit different to hear about empty towns and villages but seeing it for themselves had a sobering effect on them both.

'Let's get what we came for and go,' said Ginny a shiver going through her body. 'This is spooking me out. I know we were expecting it, but it feels as if the ghosts of all those people are here watching us.'

The small supermarket door was open, they stopped and silently looked round the outside before entering. It was unnervingly quiet and dark, but there were still tins on the shelves and clothing items hanging crookedly on hangers.

They loaded the van as quickly as they could with what they thought was most useful including clothes and cleaning products. Ginny felt a strong urge to leave as soon as possible and had come to trust these warnings.

With nobody around, no music, no people, they decided to take a different route home. The mood of the morning had dissipated and as they were driving along Ginny suddenly said 'stop! look at that field!' There was a horse on the ground and a foal by its side, a large white horse standing guard.

'We have to check they're OK,' said Ginny in an agitated voice, her hands suddenly shaking.

Josh stopped, and mumbled under his breath, 'typical Ginny, no thought for her own safety,' as Ginny jumped out, running to the field. Josh followed at a distance but could see the mare was dead and the foal was in a bad way.

Ginny was just going over to the stallion when they heard a noise coming from the barn. They looked and walked silently around the outside, darting glances around carefully as they went, fearful of what they would find. On entering the barn, they found a small child hiding in a corner. She was shaking and shivering, covered in hay, and visibly very frightened.

'What's your name?' asked Ginny in a soft voice, gently pulling the child towards her. 'Don't worry we're not going to hurt you'.

'Lilly,' said the child, in a shaky voice.

'What happened Lilly?' asked Ginny, as she held the child, whose whole body was shaking, close.

The child who Ginny guessed was about six years, said in a whisper.

'Mummy said to hide when the men came, so I hid in the hay. They came in the barn, but I was quiet, so they didn't find me, but they took my Mummy, Daddy and the cows. They had big trucks. I tried to feed the horses, but Polly died, and I couldn't lift the hay,' she burst into tears.

Ginny could see she was shaking. with cold and fear and grief. She took off her hoodie and gently helped Lilly into it.

~

'You stay with her Ginny.' said Josh I'll check the farm, he came back in fifteen minutes looking grim, 'there's no one there, no bodies but signs of a struggle the animals are gone as well,'

Ginny said softly 'Josh, I think you should take Lilly back to Hannah. She'll know what to do. Edward's Dad could take care of the foal. We could try and get it in the back of the van, it's so small. I'll ride the stallion towards home until you can come back with a horse box. I can let you know how far I get.'

'He's called Pegasus,' said Lilly in a quiet voice. 'Will baby be all right?'

'Yes,' said Ginny gently. 'Josh will take good care of you both. Come on Lilly, Josh will take you somewhere safe, and I promise you we will look for your Mummy and Daddy,' continued Ginny, taking the child's hand and strapping her safely in the front seat of the van.

They knew how much trouble they would be when they got back, but if they hadn't come the child may have died,

Ginny wasn't too fussed as she could give as good as she got.' She knew Josh could always get round his mum.

It took a while to get the foal in the van as it kept backing away from the van on shaky legs, but they tied him to a hook in the van and surrounded him with blankets and made sure nothing could fall on him.

'Can you calm him Josh, I couldn't bare it if he died?' said Ginny with a sigh.

'I didn't want this kind of adventure,' she said to herself, as she whispered to the stallion. Telling him what was happening, calmly stroking him gently all the time. She found she had the same affinity as Josh to most animals, but horses were her love.

Ginny went to the barn and found Pegasus's saddle and bridle. She fed him hay and tacked him up, thinking how lucky it was that she had taken to riding so easily. She was a natural with animals surprising herself, as she always thought of herself as a city girl, even now. How life had changed, the prickly girl who'd left London could still be offhand and had her moments she realised. She and Josh had a tight bond, and were immensely powerful together, more than most would ever comprehend.

They hadn't been tested yet, but she had a premonition that they would be soon. Something was telling her to be exceptionally cautious. *The dream team* she thought, *Josh and her. Who would have imagined it those years ago, what would her mother have thought of her now? Probably wouldn't have cared, or was dead by now of the virus, if the drugs hadn't got her first?* Ginny gritted her teeth and refused to let emotion flow for the person who had caused her, Tip, and Bel so much pain. Seeing Hannah with Josh made her understand how a real family could be.

Girl and horse seemed to be as one as they rode over the fields through a small wood and out on the top of a hill. The early evening sky had turned a pale grey. Shadows were forming, but below she could see a farm with a large barn. There were outbuildings, and smoke coming out of the farmhouse chimney in a white plume. A prickly sensation in her neck, instinctively made her pull back, quietly urging Pegasus backwards further into the vegetation, and prepared herself to wait for Josh and Val. As from behind the trees, she saw below a group of six adults and four children in the farmyard, surrounded by several men with guns.

They were being herded into a barn, some of the children were crying when a man hit one of the children with his gun. Ginny felt the fear of the small group, and the intention of the gunmen. Ginny realised as she sent out a probe One had her ability to read minds, she tried to act quickly and not panic. She withdrew her probe and blocked her mind, hoping that he'd been too busy to notice her intrusion. 'Josh, I need help urgently,' she said, sending her message explaining the situation quickly in pictures and thoughts, giving her location.

'There are ten men with guns. One at least is of Sherabar's race, he can read minds, so you need to be careful to shield your thoughts, when near.

CHAPTER TWENTY

Ginny was thankful she was in her dark top and jogger bottoms. She'd grabbed a spare hoodie from the van too, so she wasn't cold. She took out the dart gun she kept with the other items in the security belt, she and Josh always had with them. They may seem wilful and stubborn to some, but where their security was concerned Josh, and Ginny, were meticulously prepared and careful. She wanted to find out more, so rather than waiting with Pegasus she told him to stay hidden and wait. She wanted to keep him safe. Then ran down the field keeping to the hedgerow. She slowed down as she got nearer the farmyard praying there were no dogs to give her away. Stopping where she had a good viewing vantage point but couldn't be seen. Waiting to see what happened next, she wished she had her bow, but the dart gun would have to do.

She watched as the men locked the heavy door with a padlock. As far as she could see there didn't seem to be any windows or other doors. Two men were on guard outside. The others went back into the farmhouse and Ginny took the risk of entering one man's mind, taking care it wouldn't be noticed. He was not the one who had her ability to mind read. The man was relaxed which made it easier, there had been a large pot of stew already on the range and some homemade beer in the fridge. They decided to eat, drink, relax and maybe stay the night, but hadn't decided whether to kill, or take the adults with them. The children were of no use to them, but this man still had a few scruples, and wasn't sure about killing children.

'Josh, can you hear me?' Ginny sent to him. 'You need to come as quickly as possible; I'm going to have to go in soon. They're going to kill the children; can you contact Joe, and see if he is able to give you a plan of the farm-house, it could be useful.' She crouched lower and saw the two other men glance round the corner at the far end of the barn before returning to their watch stations at each end of the barn.

'These are Thor's men I'm sure, they have two large lorries one full of livestock, I can feel the animal's distress. The men don't seem to be too worried about the animal's welfare. They have guns, but not sure what other powers the one who can read minds has, so keep your minds closed and senses alert. Please hurry.'

Josh had arrived home, parked the van haphazardly, jumped out, and left the van with its contents and Lilly, with Hannah and David Edwards dad. Josh gave him charge of the foal, hoping it wasn't too late to save it. He then rushed round to see Val, calling for Ella and Lewis on the way.

Val had already been warned by Josh, and had the armoured van, equipment, Jenny, Edward, and Doug waiting, as Josh and the others jumped in.

'We're on our way,' Josh told Ginny. 'We'll be with you in thirty or thirty-five minutes if we get a move on.'

'Don't drive into the farm,' warned Ginny.

She crept nearer making note of where the guards were. *At least they're not together,* she thought as she armed her dart gun. A branch cracked under her foot making the man look up, in that instant she fired her gun, and he went down without a sound.

Crawling nearer she lifted him under his arms and dragged him round the back of a small shed. Covering him with leaves. Luckily, she was extraordinarily strong, due to her training with Sherebar when at school, so this didn't prove too much of a problem, she took his gun and the keys out of his pocket. She knew she had to deal with the other guard before doing anything else. Silently moving round to the other end of the barn she whispered, 'I'm here,' as the man looked up in surprise, she fired again, and before he could make a sound, he went down a silently as the other one.

This one was a bit harder to move but no one in the farm-house seemed to take any notice of what was going on outside, to Ginny's relief. Taking the keys, she unlocked the barn. The group inside had armed themselves with what they could find but, the barn had been well built and there was no hope they would have been able to escape.

They looked in amazement at the young woman before them. 'I'm Ginny,' she said. 'You haven't much time, help's coming, but you need to go as silently as possible up the hill to the wood and hide. My horse is up there so don't frighten him. It's essential that you all keep quiet until I say it's all clear. The children must understand this, as your lives depend on it,' she said dramatically wiping a layer of sweat from her forehead. Brushing her hair out of her eyes with her fingers. She realised she must look a mess and hoped she hadn't scared them. Whispering she continued. 'One of those men can read minds, it may seem strange, but I need you to believe me. So do not think about rescue, or where you are hiding. Keep your minds busy with thinking about animals, children, or anything else, such as telling the children stories. Go now, I'll re-lock the barn. Take these two guns,' she said giving them to two of the farmers. 'Don't use them unless it is completely necessary. I will explain all about us when this is all over.' They responded to her authority which was amazing for someone so young.

As she left, she noticed two packages on the wall picking them up with a grin she locked the barn and looked for a way to get onto the farmhouse roof without being seen.

The men were enjoying themselves in the farmhouse as the beer was flowing freely. They'd found the farm store and were lounging round the room.

Ginny sat in the apex of the roof by the chimney looking at the stars. *They don't change* she thought. *What's out there she wondered? Sherebar wasn't very forthcoming about where he came from.*

Was the virus deliberate, a way to save the world from eventual extinction?

Would she ever know? something else to ask Sherebar.

She sensed Josh and Val, near and realised they had brought the others. 'One of you let the animals out of the lorry as soon as you see the men come out.' she asked. 'They're in a bit of distress.' Being able to use telepathy had its uses.

Used to Ginny by now, they didn't question her request. Edward stood by the lorry as he was the one most familiar with farm animals.

Time for her next performance Ginny thought. 'Get ready,' she warned Josh, Val, and Jenny, and sent the packages she has picked up from the barn down the lighted chimney.

The insecticide smoke bombs caused havoc once they hit the fire. It was quite fun to watch, thought Ginny as she scampered back down to the floor.

'Typical Ginny,' commented Val to Jenny, feeling Ginny's emotion. 'To think this is fun. Clever to realise how to use those packages though. Makes it easier for us.'

~

First, there was just a bit of shouting then choking, as the men streamed out of the building. Easy picking for those waiting outside. *Good practice for Ella and Lewis,* Ginny thought.

To add to the confusion, the animals eventually freed by Edward, came stampeding round the corner. The exception was one of the men coming out of the farmhouse, he stayed calm, ignoring the chaos. He raised his gun aiming at Val, as well as sending a blast of energy towards Jenny. In that moment Ginny and Josh sent a protective wall around them both, as Josh blasted the man with his stun gun.

The man rolled slowly to the ground and lay still.

'How did you do that?' questioned Val. Then Ginny saw realisation dawn on her that there was not much, other than a bit of restraint, she could teach these two.

'I don't know,' said Josh shaking his head. 'It just happened. '

'We need to get him picked up,' said Val pointing to the man on the floor, he's too dangerous for us to take with us. The others won't wake for a while. I'll call Joe.'

Edward rounded up the loose animals and put them in a secure field, and walked up the hill to tell the farmers it was safe to come back and feed them. Jenny went to open all the farmhouse windows to let the air in.

Val looked at Ginny and Josh and told them. 'I love you

both lots and admire you, although you can be extremely irritating at times. Perhaps children like you two are the future. If so, there is a bit of hope for the world.' She continued thoughtfully. 'I worry about you, and you still have growing up to do. You give me a heart attack sometimes. But for everyone's safety you need to follow the protocols, at least some of the time.' This Val said with a smile, as she hugged them both before ushering them back to wait by the armoured car.

She was surprised when Ginny turned round and gave her a big hug, tears in her eyes. 'I love you too, Val.' Val encased Ginny in her arms and said. 'We all love you Ginny, don't ever forget that.'

CHAPTER TWENTY-ONE

'There's someone in the other lorry,' said Val as she walked towards it. 'I can feel distress but no danger.' She gingerly opened the back and saw two bundles huddled in the corner. Looking more closely there were a man and woman bound, with tape over their mouths. The woman with a nasty gash on her head and the man with cuts to his hands and arms.

'Doug, can you help?' she called. 'I've got two casualties here. One might be serious.'

Doug came running carrying his medicine bag, took one look at the woman and said, 'we need to get her inside quickly. The man needs treatment but he's not so bad. Lewis, can you help carry them inside?'

The smoke in the farmhouse had dissipated, Jenny quickly cleared the area, and they laid the woman on the table. Lewis and Josh went back to get the man.

Jenny said,' I need some sharp scissors, and could someone boil some water', She cut the bonds round their hands and legs and gently removed the tape round their mouths. The woman groaned as Jenny helped Doug clean their wounds. 'Lilly, she cried what's happened to my Lilly?'

'Don't worry,' soothed Doug, realising Lilly, the little girl with Hannah was their daughter. 'She's safe and well.' Tears filled the woman's eyes and her body sagged in relief.

Outside Edward had bought the group down followed by Pegasus. The farmers were helping him move the comatose attackers into the barn and lock the door. 'I think we should shoot them,' said one farmer his teeth barred in anger, tightly clenching his fists. 'They were going to kill us and our children.'

'Let's leave them for a minute and think about it,' said Edward. Although he completely understood their feelings. 'You should take the children inside. They could probably do with a drink and something to eat. We can have a talk about it then, and how you can protect yourself in the future.'

'Who are these people?' asked one of the women pointing to the two injured people.

'I think they were kidnapped from a farm a few miles away,' said Val. 'We'll know more later, but the horse belongs to them, Ginny and Josh rescued their daughter Lilly who was hiding. She's safe for now.'

'Who are you? Who's that amazing girl?' enquired one of the women, who said her name was Sue. 'We can't thank you enough for saving us.'

'We live in a village nearby, and Ginny sent us a message that you needed help,' explained Val, 'We'll tell you our story later, but you may find it hard to believe. We have been vaccinating farms around us, for the two years before the virus struck, so that you could survive the virus.'

'We've only been vaccinated for the flu virus, a woman came round and offered it to us all,' said Sue. As one of us had been quite ill with the flu that year, we all decided to have it. Including the children as it was offered free.'

'That would have been Hannah one of our staff. The vaccine you had was against this current virus, we weren't able to tell you the truth as we didn't want the population panicked. It was impossible to vaccinate everyone because the vaccine was so difficult to make,' said Val.

If they already had a lot to take in, the farm group were even more shaken when a small triangle shaped craft landed quietly just outside the yard. They watched open mouthed as the top lifted and a man stepped out. A weird day just got weirder.

Val and Jenny rushed outside, big smiles on their faces.

'Joe,' they said flinging their arms round him, Val and Jenny had missed their brother, not having seen him in person for months. 'What are you doing here?'

'I've come to pick up your unwelcome visitor,' he grinned, 'and thought I would pay a visit as long time no see. Josh gave me an update on your adventure.'

'Doug, Edward, Josh,' called Val as she and Jenny pulled Joe into the farmhouse. 'Look who we have here.'

Josh rushed up pulling Ginny with him. 'Joe this is Ginny.'

Joe opened his arms and gave them both a hug.

'Much better than meeting online,' Joe said with a smile. Noticing that Ginny was a bit hesitant with physical contact.

'I can't stay, as I have to get back before our prisoner wakes,' indicating the comatose man. 'I will try and visit again soon,' he promised. 'Come and help me put him in the Hawk, as we call the craft, and you can have a look at the tech inside before I go'.

Ginny held back, but her inquisitive mind was so intrigued with the craft, that she soon followed Josh. Inside was full of instruments and surprisingly spacious.

'We need one of these, Joe,' said Ginny excitedly her reticence overcome by the amazing array of tech before her. 'Think of the ground we could cover, and the adventures we could have,' she said cheekily.

Josh turned round with a grin, clearly in complete agreement.

They watched as Joe took off, doing a loop the loop then zooming away at great speed becoming invisible in a heartbeat.

'Wish we could be with you,' Josh and Ginny shouted after him. 'It could be a bit more interesting with Joe around,' commented Ginny.

The farmers were adamant that they deal with the bodies of the remaining men. They'd had to make hard choices to survive over the past two years, Val understood. They knew exactly what they were going to do, and no-one was going to stop them. There was a harbour a few miles away with plenty of empty boats. A few still working. A nice long voyage was just what these men needed.

One of the children pointed to one of the men on the ground unable to move, but still alive and said. 'That one didn't agree with killing children and wanted to try and stop it, don't know how though.'

'How do you know that?' Queried Val.

'I saw it in my mind,' the child answered.

'That's interesting,' murmured Val.

'Leave that one.' Val said to the Farmers pointing to the one the child had picked out. 'We'll take him back with us, his information could be useful.'

The farmers roughly loaded the comatose and dead into a truck, knowing that they would deal with the attackers as they saw fit. Thankful as they were for rescue, no one was going to try and kill their children and not pay for it.

CHAPTER TWENTY-TWO

Sometime after the farm attack and rescue, on what was a warm sunny day, Mrs. Taylor, Doug's adopted mother, walked down the street mopping her brow in the heat of the sun, while pushing David Joshua in his buggy, who was chattering away and laughing at Cassie walking by his side, when a stranger started approaching them.

Mrs Taylor stopped, stood very still suddenly, and fell into a trance-like state. Cassie gave a low growl but didn't seem to be able to move either.

As he got nearer the stranger said, 'Derebar I know you are there behind the woman, but you're not strong enough to stop me taking the child.'

Derebar who although a malevolent spirit, made an exception where David Joshua was concerned, replied with a laugh, and having known Luci well in his disreputable past said, 'well done Luci, I thought you may be able to feel me, but you have underestimated David Joshua and I.'

With that, a beam shot from David Joshua into Luci and a

pile of ash appeared on the floor which gradually drifted into the air.

David Joshua giggled and clapped his hands,

'Well done son,' said Derebar as he surrounded the boy in a white mist. 'You know I am always there with you. You are getting stronger, but you need to keep that hidden for now, for your own safety.'

With that the mist disappeared, Mrs. Taylor came out of her trance, noticed David Joshua giggling to himself and smiled. As Mrs Taylor walked on, she said to him, 'what's so funny David Joshua?' Then as Cassie howled, she took a quick look around a worried frown replacing her smile. 'Cassie why are you howling? that's unusual for you. There's no one there.' Then using her usual response to anything troubling. 'Shall we go to the bakers? The shops open. I don't know where your Mum and Dad have gone, but I am sure they won't be long. We can go back to your farm, and you can feed the chickens while we wait for them.'

The boy smiled at Mrs Taylor and nodded his agreement and said to Cassie, 'Cassie act as normal, what happened is our secret.' He could communicate with Cassie using his mind as well as his Mum could, but Val wasn't aware of that fact yet. Derebar secretly taught him by gradually opening his young mind. Something Val and Edward would be horrified about if they knew.

Cassie had decided after the incident with Mrs Taylor, she wanted to be back with Toby, Josh's dog, at Hannah's farm. She sat down and refused to move when Mrs Taylor had passed by, on the way home via the bakers shop to Edwards farm.

On getting back from all the drama at the survivor's farm, Val was exhausted and at Hannah's farm, slumped gratefully into one of Hannah soft chairs. She had called into Hannah's to check on Lilly, update Hannah about Lilly's parents, and pick up Cassie,

Val had left Edward behind at the survivor's farm to check on the animals, and to wait for the farmers to come back from their boat trip. Knowing him so well, she realised he wasn't going to ask the farmers what they had done with the men that attacked them. They both had an idea but would rather not know for certain.

Val let herself and Cassie into her house. Mrs Taylor leaving a message that she and David Joshua were staying to collect eggs at Edwards farm. Val couldn't face going back there just now. She didn't want to know what had happened to the attackers, but she felt they deserved whatever the farmers decided to do. The moment she shut the door she felt a relief. It was as if the house had surrounded her in warmth and a hug.

The house was cosy and still smelt of Mrs Taylor's baking. It was inviting. This was her place, her refuge. Sitting on the sofa with its bright coloured throws she put her arm around Cassie and let the tears fall. She cried for her old life and fear for the future overtook her. 'What shall I do Cass? she asked the dog, as Cassie tried to lick away the tears. 'I didn't think life would be like this, I know we are lucky here, but how I long for our past life. Now my laboratory is used for vaccine production and research, all my herbs and natural remedies are put on a back burner and I'm not sure I like living on Edwards farm. It doesn't feel like home.'

There was a knock on the door, and still shaking with emotion she wasn't going to open it when a key turned in the lock and Hannah appeared.

'Oh Val, what's the matter? I thought something was wrong when you stopped at the farm,' said Hannah putting her arms around Val.

'I don't know what I feel anymore,' said Val her shoulders shaking with grief. 'Edward and I don't see enough of our son, he's growing fast, we just spend so much time making sure everything is okay, so the village can survive. We don't see much of each other either unless there's an emergency.' She squeezed her eyes shut so more tears couldn't escape. 'I know Edward loves David Joshua, but it's hard to build up a relationship when they see so little of each other. I don't feel at home on the farm. What am I going to do, Hannah?'

Hannah sighed. 'Firstly, you need to talk to Edward. If he doesn't know there's a problem, he can't do anything to help, can he? You need to make a part of the farm into your space and perhaps spend a bit more time here. Give yourself a break. You can't do everything yourself Val. Have you talked to Jenny about how you feel?' Releasing Val, Hannah got up to go and make a herbal tea to calm Val's nerves and grief. Her face showing her concern.

Rocking backwards and forwards in her chair Val murmured to herself. 'I have to be careful to keep a block on this, Joe and Jenny have enough to contend with without worrying about me.'

Just then there was another knock on the door. Hannah went to open it and was faced with Edward at the door.

'Can you ask Mrs Taylor to stay and look after David Joshua at home farm.' he whispered to Hannah kissing her on the cheek, 'I think I'm needed here.'

Hannah nodded, and slipped out whispering to herself, that it was sad that so much pressure was on the shoulders of so few.

Edward went straight to Val pulled her into his arms and held her tight. 'I thought there was something wrong and knew you would be here.' He said as he stroked her hair. 'Nothing's so bad that we can't work it out together. Do you still love me?' he asked seriously.

'Yes,' said Val without hesitation, making her realise that unhappy as she was, that was still the truth.

'You don't like living at the farm, do you? He said sadly. 'What can I do to make it feel more like home, or do you want to stay here? I can't leave the farm because of the animals, but I want to be with you, too.'

Val's breathing returned to normal as she felt their energy join, in the comfort of his arms and replied softly. 'Can you stay here tonight? I need to stay here but would like you to stay too, and perhaps tomorrow when I'm not so emotional we can work something out.' Edward gently took her hand, and they went upstairs together.

In a bedroom at his own farm a small boy was visualising his parents together, gave a little smile and went to sleep. One day he would have to tell them of his abilities but not just yet.

CHAPTER TWENTY-THREE

The Government was still functioning, although much smaller now, and had spent most of the last two years dealing with the many bodies caused by the virus. Apart from anything else it caused a health hazard, and usual means of burial weren't available. Crematoriums were running twenty-four hours a day and staffing was a problem, as were the black clouds it generated. It had been overwhelming, the smell of death terrible, and hospitals that were still operating as normal were dealing with excess illnesses because of the situation. Although there was fewer people, they still needed looking after.

Parks and nearby fields had been dug up for mass graves. There were no mourners, services, or music, only a heavy feeling of loss and despair. The surviving population were shell-shocked, as most had lost someone they loved. Critical workers and their families had been a priority for the vaccine available, but an age limit was put on these workers and families, except in exceptional circumstances. So those over seventy were scarce unless immune. A lot of useful knowledge had died with them.

In London, empty high-rise blocks were desolate and dark not a soul moving, no noise, except for the sound of birds reclaiming their territory in unkempt gardens, and, in empty parks Foxes and Badgers roamed at will, pets left behind survived the best they could on the detritus left behind of those who came before.

Those of the population that survived, had quickly moved to empty accommodation in the more prosperous parts of town, around green spaces, near the river, and survived on what they could scavenge and food drops by the authorities still in charge. The enterprising were using abandoned allotments to grow food. Green spaces were emerging and wildflowers thriving so there was some light beginning to shine amongst all the desolation. Chickens could be heard crowing and birdsong greeted the rising sun. The Government had managed to keep sporadic electric, water and sewerage going with the help of the army and vaccinated key workers. It wasn't all darkness and doom. People were finding skills they hadn't realised they had, and some small business ventures were beginning to thrive.

In an underground bunker, a small group of men and women sitting round a table were discussing the current situation. The man who seemed to be in charge, called Jack Reed, said solemnly. 'You know the decisions we had to make about the vaccine, we just didn't have enough. Even with the knowledge of past pandemics. Plus, there were other forces in play, like Thor, against us, that fought us all the way. It's as if they can predict what we are doing. We managed to vaccinate the group that we thought could help everyone survive and keep our nuclear installations safe, but we are unsure how other countries used their supply of vaccine.'

'How dangerous is that for us?' asked one woman. 'A nuclear site or missiles not safely controlled, could lead to a situation worse than we have now.'

'All heads of nuclear countries had agreed to decommission their weapons and protect their power installations, but how many did, I don't know.' said Jack. 'I don't know how well trained the staff were. That could be a problem.'

'Did we comply, are our installations safe? Did we disarm our weapons?' queried another.

Jack looked uncomfortable but eventually answered. 'No, we didn't have time to disarm them, but they have been made safe.'

'So, we not only have to contend with the aftermath of the virus but the nuclear situation as well,' said one of the women present angrily. 'Do we have contact with anyone in these countries. Do we know how they fared?'

'We think Nuclear power sites are protected. If there had been a meltdown we would know by now. Personnel at these sites were a priority for vaccination. It's not something any country, if they wanted to survive would neglect. Just think what happened in Chernobyl and Japan,' said Jack.

'With regards to Thor, they have two sites that we know of here, but could have more, they are also active in other countries especially Africa and America. Originally, we thought they just wanted to be first with a vaccine to make money, and they tried to steal ours, but now it looks like world domination is their aim.'

He continued feeling uncomfortable as his body tensed with stress. 'Another group lead by a mysterious man called Sherebar, diverted some of Thor's deliveries to our facilities. We think this group have developed their own vaccine and were following their own vaccinating criteria that included farmers, fishermen, and families, but we are not sure. They are secretive, and we don't know where they operate from. They have been sending us highly useful information on the locations and operation of Thor.'

'Why was this vaccine so hard to produce, surely the knowledge and speed we produced vaccines for past pandemics must have helped?' enquired a small rotund man. His tapping foot betraying his anxiety.

'We only had a small amount of virus to work with. It was extremely unusual. We found out by accident, that a few prospectors in Australia, and some in our own population who were found to be immune, had a constituent of their blood, that, when added to our vaccine made it work,' said Jack looking around at the concerned faces before him. 'But even then, it was difficult to produce enough to use. Finding those willing to help us around the world by giving blood meant testing large numbers, and that took time.' Jack explained, to try to make his colleagues understand the difficulties encountered.

'So, what is the situation now, and how do we manage it?' asked Rachel his deputy. 'This should be our priority.'

'Food stores are secure for another two years, and the Government can continue to distribute food. We need to start finding ways to contact any surviving food producers, and be self-sufficient within that time,' said Jack. Trying to stop himself fidgeting in his chair. 'Most transport is electric, but drivers are short. There are no planes flying or cargo ships for the same reason. Fuel and electric shortages don't help us in trying to rebuild our life. We have been collecting and storing all useful items to use as replacements or for repairs,' said Jack. 'Luckily, we learnt from past pandemics to bring back a lot of manufacturing here and are self-sufficient in many areas, if we can find the raw materials and the survivors with the knowledge, to take over manufacturing.'

'Do we know how many survived and do we need to re vaccinate, if so, how soon, and do we have supplies?' asked one of the others.

'We do now have enough vaccine to revaccinate our population. From those we have retested there are still antibodies two years later but there is a slight reduction. There may still be some virus hidden in pockets around the world we just don't know.' Jack looked down at the floor and paused, trying to calm his fast-beating heart, before continuing. 'The figures available are grim. From the amount of bodies, we've had to deal with, we think well under twenty percent of the population here survived and this contains children. It could be much lower in other parts of the world,' answered Jack. 'Also, it seems from reports available from hospitals still operating, that no children have been born in hospital, if not conceived before the virus arrived. The earth is having its revenge,' he said wryly.

'Is there any good news,' asked one of the group.

'Yes,' answered Jack positively. 'There is, as the operating farms we know of were already automated, with equipment solar powered or electric. They are producing a good quantity of crops. This is enabling us to build up some surplus. The group led by this man called Sherebar had the foresight to vaccinate all of the seed bank staff and scientists. Ensuring we can restock the arable farms. We now have no debt, there are no mortgages, and we can reset our finance system using the gold reserves we have. Realistically collecting tax is not possible yet.' He took a big breath and smiled. 'We have the chance to make the country work for everyone if you all have the will to do it.'

CHAPTER TWENTY-FOUR

The shed was dark with one sink and toilet in the corner, it smelt damp and the only light had been turned off. Six children were sitting on mattresses on the floor. Two girls and four boys, three silently shaking with sobs. Andy knew that they were tired, hungry, and frightened. He was twelve years old but small for his age, and berating himself for getting into this situation, he thought of himself as streetwise, but having lost all those that were dear to him, and fending for himself and his little group for months, he had been caught off guard as he was tired and stressed, So when the official looking bus came round saying that the Government was finding orphan children to look after, feed, and educate, showing pictures of where they would be staying, which was large house with big gardens, he had seen it as a solution to his problem of keeping his friends safe and fed. Unfortunately, he soon learned of his mistake.

They were taken to a grey block building in a compound, wire fencing all around. Nothing like the building they were shown in the picture when they got onto the bus. All were given the same grey uniform to wear, it consisted of a top and loose trousers. Anyone who objected soon learned to obey commands. He often saw children battered and bruised.

All the children were put to work for six hours each day fitting small pieces of metal together. They didn't know what they were for. It was monotonous and they were not allowed to stop, except for a toilet break. They were fed just enough to keep them alive and had to do an hour of exercise every day shouting slogans they didn't understand. There was also an hour of learning after work was done, anyone good at maths mysteriously disappeared, so Andy told other children to get those wrong.

They were all so tired and terrified, not really understanding what was happening to them. No one rebelled, as any who did were strapped into the dreaded chair. Not something they would want to repeat. You could hear the screams of anyone unfortunate enough to be strapped in it blocks away. This group had been there several weeks and were starting to feel the effects on their bodies. Some of the children just disappeared from the workhouses. *We need to find a way out soon,* Andy thought.

Andy ever watchful, had noted that one of the guards was not always as careful as others in locking the door each night, He probably thought no one would dare to try and escape after what had happened to the last two who'd tried. Andy kept this to himself until it had happened a couple of times. He had also taken careful note of their surroundings and noticed a Badger hole under one of the fences. He thought they could get out through it if they were careful. They wouldn't be missed until the next morning. He knew exactly where they should head to.

If they could make it out, they may stand a chance of escape. Taking all six of them was a risk, but he couldn't leave them behind. They were his family now, he thought steadfastly. He hadn't thought of himself as brave until he arrived here. Now it was a matter of survival of the fittest, or smartest. He was determined to get as many of his hut out as possible. This place was a living hell with its dirt, smell, and atmosphere of fear.

The chance came two weeks later. He told the others they must be incredibly quiet, not to speak, but to follow him. Even the youngest one at nine understood the danger. They all promised to do as Andy said. He understood very well the poor kids were very frightened, malnourished, and jumped at the slightest sound.

Andy carefully opened the door and peered out. All was quiet, but the moon was shining, making escape that much more dangerous. They crept round the building and kept closely together, Andy quickly found the badger hole and pushed the smallest one through first. They followed one by one. Luckily Andy was small and thin as well.

Andy put his hand to his mouth indicating to be very quiet, as they could hear a rustling very near. He held his breath hoping they weren't going to be discovered when a large Badger ambled along the path. 'Come 'he whispered to the others. We have a long way to go. We must walk along the road, and I don't want to meet anyone unexpectedly.'

They trudged along for two miles the younger ones already getting tired, when they came upon an abandoned car in the road. Andy quickly looked through the window holding his hand up for the others to wait. He saw the keys still in the ignition, he directed them round the other side of the car and opened the door for them to pile in, it was a bit squashed, but they didn't care. Noticing the decomposed body on the other side of the car. He hoped death had come quickly, having seen these many times before. This was not a sight he wanted the other children to encounter.

He was thankful that his brother had taken him joy riding at the beginning of the trouble, and taught him to drive, he still missed him very much, but he'd gone out one day and never came back. Andy didn't know if he would ever see him again. His Mum, Dad and Grandma were all gone. He couldn't think too much about it, as it hurt too much. The others had all lost their parents but luckily, they had found each other. His stomach cramped whenever he thought about his family. They had to make new families now.

They all had to grow up in the past two years, and with wisdom that belied his age, Andy said to himself. 'We need and deserve a bit of good luck now.'

Andy turned the key, and to his delight the engine started, he noticed there was still fuel in the tank, being what was considered an old-fashioned car nowadays, as it still used fuel. They sped along the empty road with the cars dimmed lights showing the way, not turning off until they came to the sign for a small Harbour. There were several boats bobbing in the water, still waiting for their owners to use them. It was a ghostly sight. There was a slight breeze, and the clinking of the boats the only sound.

No one was about, the two shops were dark and empty, but the moon gave Andy enough light to check out the small craft. His Dad had been a keen sailor and Andy had been sailing here many times, the boats had been small, but he knew how to rig a sail and steer a course. He loved the sea and cherished the memory of his Dad. It was all he had left.

Getting them all in the boat he had chosen, took some time, as some of the children were quite scared of the jump it took to get in the boat, and were spooked when it rocked. To Andy's relief there were life jackets in the small cabin. Which was helpful as only four of them could swim.

After making sure these were securely fitted, Andy unhooked the rope tethering the boat and used the pole in the boat to push it away from its mooring. There was a slight breeze and as Andy unfurled the sail the wind took it, and he steered it out into open water.

'Where are we going?' asked one of the young boys with a tremor in his voice.

I wish I knew thought, Andy as he said, 'as far away as possible,'

He sailed where the wind took him, some of the children fell asleep lulled by the sounds of the sea. Andy tried to keep the boat in sight of the shore as he knew they would have to land somewhere. They were all hungry and needed food. He just hoped it was far enough away from their captors to keep them all safe.

CHAPTER TWENTY-FIVE

Wilf had been a music producer and songwriter, his wife Maggie a singer. YouTube and social media had made them rich and famous, and they toured the world with many well-known bands. They enjoyed themselves and didn't give much thought to the future as they had a son, and their life seemed complete. Then an unwary remark caused a media frenzy and all the work they had done helping young artists was forgotten. Their songs not played, and friends disappeared. The remark had been taken out of context and no amount of explaining made any difference.

As the furore was affecting their son, they sold up in London and moved to the small village of Wellasea in the southeast of England where they now lived. The house was old and rambling but had outbuildings suitable for a studio and a barn they hoped to use for events, when all the hysteria had died down.

The garden although ramshackle had a stream, a well, orchard, and small wood. It was also near the sea so that Wilf could indulge his love of fishing and Maggie her art. It had surprised them how much they enjoyed their life and the extra time they could spend with their son. He wasn't musical or arty but loved the countryside and became an expert on the natural world as he grew up. He met his wife when traveling to Australia and now had two children of his own.

For Wilf and Maggie, older now, the virus had been devastating and they had no word from their son or grandchildren. They just hoped they were safe. There were many empty houses in the village now, but there were also some complete families that had survived including themselves. Foraging and fishing had kept them alive so far, but two families had left hoping to find an easier life in other parts of the country. Wilf thought it better to cope with what they had than to risk another unknown.

Most of the village had been vaccinated for flu by the mobile clinic that visited one day to the annoyance of one of the local doctors who wasn't expecting it. Was that a factor in their survival, Wilf wondered? News was scarce but the word that did reach them, didn't have good news. They had to bury many in the village, the distress this caused was still with him.

Wilf decided to go fishing as this relaxed him, he had found a local farm, in his wanderings, near the village, with a group of farmers that had milk, butter and other vegetables. He swapped his fish and news with them and had been disturbed to learn they had recently been attacked but were helped by a young woman, and others with what seemed unusual powers. They didn't want to talk about it, but it made Wilf anxious for their own village's safety. He warned his village survivors to be extra careful and keep their children close.

Walking to the harbour he marvelled at how nature was

repairing itself and how loud the morning chorus was now. Weeping willows lined the road and self-sown wheat was growing in the neglected fields. He felt nature was something to be grateful for and gave it a helping hand whenever he could. Birdsong was louder than he had noticed before, and the owl living in his oak tree called to his mate every evening lifting the spirits of Maggie and himself. It wasn't all bad he had good friends at the farm and his village. He loved his home and Maggie was great company and the love of his life. Despite everything he was content.

There weren't many boats in the harbour, but most were still being used. At least the fish were plentiful and a good source of food. The village still had a store of fuel. Wilf also had solar power, and his nets were in good condition as he had always been meticulous in his care of his boat, his pride and joy.

After he'd been fishing for a while and getting ready to head home, he noticed a small sailing boat that seemed stationary by the headland, what's that doing there, he wondered, as he decided whether to investigate. In the end his curiosity got the better of him and he turned the boat round. Taking the gun he always took with him from its hiding place, after the conversation with the farmers. He slowly approached the boat with caution. 'Hi there,' he called, as he approached, 'do you need help? 'Getting closer he saw six small bodies clinging together.

The eldest stood up and seeing there was one only one man in the boat. shouted. 'We need help, are you from Thor?'

'Who's Thor?' queried Wilf.

'They're after us,' replied the boy.

'If I throw you a rope can you secure it?' asked Wilf. 'I think it will be too dangerous to try and get you all on board here. I can tow you to the harbour'.

Andy turned to the others who were now bedraggled,

hungry and frightened. 'We must chance this; do you all agree?' he asked the others, who nodded their agreement. 'Throw the rope.' Andy shouted.

It took a while to secure everything, and Wilf was careful manoeuvring his boat and slowly towed them to the harbour. One of the other boats was getting ready to go out and the two men jumped out onto the quay to help Wilf secure the small boat and transfer the children to safety.

As they stood shivering on the quayside Maggie drew up in their van after having received a prearranged distress signal from Wilf. 'Where are you from and what are your names?' she asked the children, gently wrapping them in blankets always stored in the van.

'I'm Andy,' said the oldest boy, 'and these are my friends and family. We were kidnapped and made to work by someone called Thor. They said we were going to a big house where we would be looked after. I should have known better but was so tired of scavenging.' His lip started to quiver as he tried to hold back his tears. 'My Mum and Dad disappeared and my brother, who was looking after me went out and didn't come back. I met these when looking for food, their families were gone too. We were kept in sheds, so they are my family now and they stay with me.'

'Let's get you home and some food and warm clothes and we can decide together what we should do,' said Maggie.' I'll make sure you stay together.'

'We're not going back,' warned Andy as one of the others began to cry.

'No, you are not going back,' agreed Maggie with conviction, 'but we need to talk to someone who can make sure you stay safe.' Two hours later they were back at Wilf and Maggie's' house, their uniforms burnt and clothes from the bundle Maggie had been gathering in case her grandchildren ever visited, distributed. Clearly distressed the children huddled together and flinched if touched. Once the children had been fed with soup, homemade bread and put to bed, all in one room refusing to be separated, Maggie went to join Wilf.

Andy had stayed up telling Wilf the whole story of how they had escaped. 'I need to take you to a nearby farm tomorrow,' said Wilf. 'They will help to keep you safe, and they may know those who can help. Will you trust me?'

'I don't have much choice, do I?' answered Andy abruptly. Then he hung his head, because he knew in his heart Wilf was only trying to help, but he was tired and scared, his body still shivering when he thought how lucky they were to escape. 'Thor kill those that try to escape, we've all heard the screams, and it gives us nightmares.'

'You try and sleep now; we'll talk more in the morning,' said Wilf gently, understanding how brave this small group was to have escaped. Once they were all asleep Wilf asked Maggie. 'What do you think, is it true or a fantasy?'

'I think it's the truth, they were traumatised. I want them to stay here and look after them. We have the room. I need to do this Wilf, but after what Andy's told us we need help to keep them, and us safe. It's quite frightening what they've been through,' answered Maggie. 'I feel this is a gift we've been given, they will bring life back to the village.'

The next morning the children looked much better but were still very scared. 'We won't let anyone hurt you,' said Maggie as she fed them scrambled eggs from her hens, for breakfast, 'I would like you all to stay with us, but Andy is going with Wilf this morning to see if we can get more help. Are you happy to stay with me?'

'It's okay' said Andy to the others, 'you are safe here, but you must stay indoors. I will be back, I promise you.'

One of the girls called Elly asked in a soft, shaky voice. 'Will I ever see my Mum and Dad again.'

'I don't know my darling,' said Maggie her heart breaking with sadness. 'We will have to see.' She just hoped if her grandchildren were in the same circumstances, someone would take them in too. She would make life better for these children starting now.

CHAPTER TWENTY-SIX

Wilf and Andy took the van and a basket of fresh fish and drove the hour it took to get to the farm. Andy hadn't spent much time in the countryside, and it seemed endless to him. He realised the sea currents must have taken the boat a good way from the camp they were held, and that made him feel a bit more secure. He had the feeling he could trust Wilf but was still wary. Andy could see buildings in the distance and the fields around looked cared for, he could hear a machine noise in the distance.

Wilf stopped halfway down a hill and waited.

'Why are we stopping?' asked Andy feeling anxious, his hands shaking.

'If we go any further an alarm will sound,' said Wilf. 'The farmers will see me here on their monitors, and someone will come to take us down. I found that out when I came first time and set their alarms off. I was surrounded by people with guns. Not what I expected. Once they realised, I wasn't a threat, and had just bought fish to exchange, I was welcomed, and they have become good friends. They have children and one, I think, you will get on well with,'

'I can't see any cameras or equipment,' queried Andy.

'No, you won't it's well hidden, said Wilf. 'Here they come,' as a ramshackle old truck came up the road. 'Hi Rick,' said Wilf to a large man in rough clothes and a big hat. 'I've bought some fish and a visitor. Also, I need a talk to you all.'

'Sounds ominous,' said Rick, 'follow me and we'll get you a drink and we can talk.'

They followed the truck down the hill and stopped in front of the farmhouse.

A woman called Sue came out of the house rubbing her hand on her apron before giving Wilf a hug. 'And who is this?' she asked smiling at Andy.

'Andy,' said Wilf, 'and this is why I wanted to talk to you, we need some help, and I wondered if you are still in touch with the group that helped you.'

'Yes, we are, come in, I'll get you a hot drink and perhaps some cake, while Rick calls the others. Lilly and her Mum and Dad are here too, so we can all hear the story together. Timmy needs to be here too, I'll call him.' Said Sue.

'Timmy you're needed,' Sue called up the stairs as she handed a drink of hot chocolate to Andy.

Chocolate, thought Andy *where did they find that?* Andy looked round the room, it was cluttered with books and toys, but was clean and homely, a pot was bubbling on the stove, washing hanging from the ceiling on a rack. The smell of the cooking making his stomach rumble. Just as he was thinking that a large piece of cake was put before him. For the first time in a long while he thought there may be a bit of hope for him, and his friends.

A boy came running down the stairs coming to an abrupt halt when he saw Andy. Andy felt a weird sensation in his head and looked at Timmy with confusion. 'You have it too,' said Timmy, 'it's just not awake yet.'

'Have what?' said Andy.

'Let's wait until the others are here and I'll explain,' answered Timmy as he accepted a drink and cake from his mum. 'This is yummy, Mum,' Timmy said with a grin as he took a large bite. The others living on the farm trouped in, including several children in mismatched clothes, who looked at Andy with interest.

'Do you feel up to telling your story Andy?' asked Wilf. 'We need to start with that. You are among friends here so don't be worried about what you say.'

Andy looked around. It was all a bit daunting and emotional, but his intuition was telling him he could trust them, so taking a gulp of his drink he started speaking.

When he had finished, Rick said, 'that was brave of you Andy, Wilf and Maggie will make sure you are all okay, but I agree with Wilf, you need help to keep you all safe. We have experienced what these Thor people can do, and it wasn't pleasant, I think it's the same organisation who attacked us, that kidnapped you. We had help from a group run by a man called Sherebar. They also rescued Lilly and her Mum and Dad,' he continued pointing them out to Andy. The little girl smiled shyly at Andy and said, 'Ginny and Josh took me to their home and then came here for Mummy and Daddy.'

'We need to contact Sherebar or Joe,' said Timmy, 'they need to know about this.'

'You'll have to do it Timmy, it'll be quicker,' said his mum. 'The training they've been giving you is going to be useful now. It's a strange world we're living in, when one of your children can communicate with someone without seeing or speaking to them,' she mused to those listening around her.

CHAPTER TWENTY-SEVEN

Sherebar and his companions had been sent to this world with the knowledge of the future virus, many centuries in the past. They had seeded the world with ideas throughout time until the world had the technology and skills to survive. Having seen the good and bad of humans they could have left the world to destroy itself, but they had descendants living here, and these could be the saviours of the new world order.

In Sherebar's underground Facility, Joe, Val, and Jenny's brother, alongside Sally, his wife, and several of Sherebar's race, were working on ways to stop the expansion of Thor around the devastated world. They had been helping survivors where possible, and Joe was busy with a programme to help farmers utilise the equipment they still had. Suddenly he received a message from Timmy, at the farm he had visited, when it was attacked by Thor, some time ago.

Joe had picked up a comatose man working for Thor, at Rick and Sue's farm when it was attacked by several of Thor's men. This man had been a useful source of inside information on Thor's organisation. Now it looked as if Timmy had gathered some more to add to that. Timmy is getting better at this, Joe thought as he received Timmy's telepathic message. He called Sherebar and the others. 'Can we get an image screen, to the farm?' asked Joe. 'We all need to hear what this young lad called Andy has to say.'

At the farm Timmy told Wilf and Andy, 'they're sending a screen, we just have to wait. We need to clear a wall first.' They all sat facing the wall in anticipation. Andy and Wilf not knowing what to expect.

Suddenly the air stilled, and a figure appeared as a hologram in the room. 'Hallo Andy and Wilf, I am Sherebar, don't be alarmed, I'm here to help. I want you to tell your story, Andy, every detail you can remember is important if we are to help you, Timmy said you have the same ability he has, so we will speak again when you are settled.'

As Andy looked startled, he continued. 'Don't be worried about it, Timmy will explain when this meeting is over, and help you slowly unlock your abilities. I hope in the future you will both be able to visit me, but in the meantime, I will send a teacher for you both.' With that the image disappeared, and a room filled with people showed on a screen, which seemed to magically download on the wall. Many of them looked like the man Sherebar they had just seen.

Then a young man appeared on the screen, he looked at his colleagues, waiting for them to settle down, before beginning. 'Hi Andy,' he said. 'I'm Joe, can you start with where you lived and what happened to you? Sherebar just told you every detail is important. We have plenty of time so don't rush.'

Andy took a deep breath getting ready to tell his story again. He told them about his family, his Mum and Dad disappearing, and his brother looking after him, teaching him to drive and scavenge. Then after several weeks of food finding, his brother going out and then disappearing. How he survived with his young friends, and why they got on the bus.

Andy said he thought they were taken by Thor to a place near Ipswich, as this was the harbour he took the boat from, having visited with his dad several times. He told what the conditions were like in the factory and the shed. He gave them a description of what they worked on, and what he remembered of the layout of the camp.

'Did you see any adults there?' asked Joe, his voice showing the concern he had, for the ordeal a brave boy had been through.

'Only guards,' said Andy. 'But I think some were there, as I heard the guards talking about putting stinging cuffs on some men and laughing about it.

'How big was the workplace, and do you know the age of the youngest there?'. asked Joe with an encouraging smile.

'The factory or shed I was in had a hundred children, so was quite big, I counted them one day, and I think the youngest was about eight. We were putting small bits of metal together, but they left the doors of a big hanger open one day and there was a large round object in there, bigger than a plane. One guard got really shouted at, for leaving the door open,' said Andy.

'Interesting,' agreed Joe. 'I need to see you, how do you feel about that, perhaps Timmy could be there too?'

Wilf interrupted, seemingly overwhelmed by Sherebar appearing, and the technology being used. 'How soon could you come? I want to make sure they stay safe, but any help would be welcome.'

'Now we know about you, we will be monitoring your area, but it may be an idea for you all to move to the farm for a few days until I get there. Would that be ok Rick?' asked Joe.

'We can put them in the home farm cottages, there would be room for them all, and the children would like some more playmates. What do you think Sue?' enquired Rick, to his wife.

'I'm fine with it, what about you?' Sue said, turning to the others sat round the table.

'Ok with us,' said one, 'We all need to help each other.'

'Can Ginny and Josh come too?' said Timmy 'I'd like to see them again.

'I'll ask,' said Joe smiling at how popular those two young people seemed to be. 'I'd like to see them too. Thanks Andy.' Joe said 'You've given us some good information. I must go now but I will see you next week'.

He waved, and the screen slowly disappeared.

'Are you sure it will be all right for us to stay with you. I don't want to put you out?' enquired Wilf. 'Or in danger, but it would be good to have company and the children need to have time to feel safe again.'

'Joe and his friends helped us out when we needed it. They saved our lives and put in our security system,' answered Sue. 'It was so scary when those men came to the farm. They were going to kill us.'

The farmers round the table nodded in agreement They shook Wilfs hand as they stood up to disperse. They liked Wilf and were happy for him to stay.

'We had better start back then,' said Wilf as he got ready to go. 'Just a thought, we have two other families living in the village, would we be able to bring them as well? They could be a bit vulnerable on their own, knowing the current situation, or at least until we know how to protect ourselves, and what we're up against.'

'Yes', said Rick, 'the children will be quite happy to have more playmates, it's been a bit boring for them stuck here all the time. We could do with a bit more help in the fields now, to be honest, and sometimes the children help with fruit and veg picking, especially if it's in the strawberry plot.'

~

'As they headed back home,' Andy said, 'that was fun Wilf, I'm sorry if us being with you causes any problems.'

'Don't worry about that Andy, we love having you and hope you will stay with us, don't ever think you're a problem, Maggie is in her element. We have a lot to think about. I need to keep you all safe, these people have been through a lot too. I think they will be a great help to us.' said Wilf with a frown, as he thought of the problems ahead. He liked the farmers and was looking forward to more company. He remembered the old saying, a problem aired was a problem shared. So true he thought.

'Do you feel able to tell me what happened in the beginning and when your parents and brother went missing?' asked Wilf. 'It was a bit hard to take everything in when you were telling that man called Joe.'

'I'll try.' said Andy. 'We all stayed in as we were asked to do and had food for two weeks. It was very scary as there were people lying in the street Mum and Dad pulled the curtains and told us not to look out. It was so hard and quite frightening. The smell was getting bad and no others in the street seemed to have survived. In the end they took it in turns to go out and find food in the empty shops.'

'One day they decided to go out together as they could bring more back with them. Food was getting harder to find, but they didn't come back. We were worried and scared, my brother and I waited, and waited, but they'd vanished. My brother took over the food finding and sometimes took me out with him, we found cars charged up, or with fuel and my brother taught me to drive. That was quite a lot of fun, but he must have been worried that something could happen to him too.' He fidgeted in his seat as if it was hard to keep retelling his story.

'We didn't see anyone in the streets, the bodies had disappeared somehow, and there didn't seem to be anyone in charge. No one about. One day he told me to stay at home and went out to have a look around, try and find Mum and Dad. He thought perhaps we should move out of the town, but he didn't come back, just like Mum and Dad.' Andy took a deep breath as his despair at remembering what he'd lost, made him sad.

'I was frightened and stayed in on my own for a few days but then went out to see if I could find food and anyone around and found these other children, they were in a quite a bad way all on their own.'

'I took them back to the house, but when we went out scavenging, we all went together. We managed quite well for a while, but it was getting harder to do. I was worried how we would manage in the future. Then when the bus came round saying it was from the Government and they would put us in safe housing, we were stupid and believed them.' Andy paused. 'It was very frightening, we were put in large huts. Anyone that cried or complained was punished. I don't think I can talk about this anymore, his voice shaking, I'm so glad we found you.'

'I'm happy you found us too,' said Wilf putting his arm round Andy's shoulder. 'We missed our family and grandchildren, and don't know if they are okay or not. You are all very welcome and we would like you to be part of our family.'

They drove along in silence, Andy looking out of the window feeling so relieved they had found Wilf and Maggie. He grieved for his mum, dad, and brother, but knew he had to make a new life, as the old one was gone forever. He was angry inside and knew he would do what he could to fight these people. At least now he had someone he felt he could trust and was hopeful the new people he had met, could help him someday to find his mum, dad, and brother.

Maggie was waiting for them as they drew up outside the house. She gave Andy a big hug as he got out of the car, knowing he was distressed and said, 'there's some sandwiches and apple juice waiting for you inside. The other children are all so excited to think we are going on another adventure together. Wilf told me all about the farm and to get some things together for a stay.'

'If you sort the children out Maggie, I'll go and talk to the other families to see what they want to do. I think it would be safer if they do come with us, at least until we know what the chances of these Thor people finding us here. We'll be safer and stronger together, said Wilf. 'You should have seen that man, Maggie, He came out of nowhere and was so calm and confident. I don't know where he was from, but I think he can help us.'

The children looked happy at the thought of meeting other children, although their eyes were darting about, as they were a bit scared too. So much had happened to them in their short life that they clinged on to Maggie. She was determined to keep them close and give them as many good new experiences as possible. It wasn't hard to imagine what the current situation was doing to so many young lives.

Maggie and Wilf packed the van with food, bedding, and some toys Maggie had found in the deserted toy shop. Luckily there had been no bodies in the toy shop as the couple who owned it didn't live there. Wilf and the other men from the surviving two families had the terrible job of burying many friends and acquaintances. It was something they'd never forget. How her and Wilf had survived she didn't know. It had scared them all. Making them more determined to make something of any life they had left.

Wilf came back with a big smile on his face. 'Not long now,' he said. 'The other fishermen, Peter, and Trev, just want to secure their boats. But both are up for anything to help keep the kids safer. They were worried when I told them what had happened to our lot. They want to meet other survivors too.'

Maggie replied. 'My priority is keeping our children safe as well. I'll get them all in the van so we're ready to go.'

~

Andy listening to all this, said to himself. 'Maggie said our children, so she must mean us to stay here. It's such a relief not to have such a responsibility on my own.' Although he knew in his heart he would have carried on if Wilf hadn't found them. It was like having grandparents. He'd never met his. He just wished his Mum, Dad and Brother were still here. 'Where are you?' He said to himself 'Will I ever see you again?' His eyes filled with tears although he tried to hide them.

Maggi saw his distress and walked over gave him a hug and whispered, 'we'll get over this Andy, and we will look for your Mum and Dad.' It will take time and we may not find them, but I promise we will try.' Andy hugged her back fiercely, deriving comfort from her enclosing arms.

Wilf came over and said, 'let's get going then,' and off they went. the other van, and people carrier following on behind.

CHAPTER TWENTY-EIGHT

The roads were empty, and it was sad passing by the unkempt fields, deserted houses and orchards bursting with unpicked fruit.

'We'll have to spend the day here.' said Maggie pointing to the fruit. 'Surely, we must be able to use some of that. I've loads of old jam jars in the shed, and we need to have lots of stores for winter.'

'We'll help,' shouted one of the children. 'I like jam.'

Maggi smiled to herself. They were recovering fast.

As they passed the more tended fields, Andy said to the other children, 'we're nearly at the farm,' and began to feel a bit better.

They came to the hill as before and waited to be given the word to continue. Wilf having warned the others what would happen. As soon as they were given the okay, they drove down to the farmyard to be met by a group of adults and several children.

'Welcome, it's so great to see others who have survived,' said farm owner Sue when Wilfs group had all arrived. 'We need to share our stories so that we know what we should do next, and how we can support each other. We know of another village where many of the villagers survived but haven't met any others except for Wilf.' She smiled suddenly and it lit up her face. 'There's a group in that village that helped us when we needed it and saved a child and her family when they were attacked. We'll tell you all about it when we've shown you the cottages. It may be a bit cramped but I'm sure you can manage for a few days.' The children were introduced to each other and sped off to feed the animals. Andy stayed behind waiting to see Timmy, who he met last time.

'Come up Andy,' called Timmy, 'I'm in the room opposite the top of the stairs.' Andy came into a typical boy's bedroom, posters on the wall, and a mess of clothes on the floor. Timmy said, 'sit on the bed and chill.'

'Have you still got the Internet?' asked Andy, 'I thought it was all gone,'

'Yes, we have it here,' said Timmy,' Joe and the people who came to help us, fixed it up so we could all communicate. 'Although it is possible for me to communicate with them another way, by using my mind, and I think you could be able to do that too.' Bouncing up and down on the bed, making Andy laugh.

'It may seem a bit frightening at first, but it's quite fun when you know what to do. You need to know how to protect yourself though and must be careful not to go into someone's mind without permission, unless it's for your or others safety.' 'I'm thinking of something, see if you know what it is.'

'I can't,' said Andy, scrunching his face up and closing his eyes.

'Yes, you can,' replied Timmy, 'Try again. Just sit still and open your mind. '

Suddenly Andy said. 'You wish you could watch football.'

'You got it,' shouted Timmy jumping up and down. 'My friends Ginny and Josh will help you when they come. They're great. It's so exciting to have a friend my age who can do the same. I feel a bit lonely being the only one here able to do it, and it's hard to shut out the noise until you understand what's going on,' he said catching his breath. 'Mum and Dad don't understand it at all. You're not supposed to go into someone's mind without permission. The wanting to do it anyway, is a bit hard sometimes.' He smiled at Andy suddenly. 'Don't think about it now. It just takes a bit of time. Let's go out and see the horses, or Mum will rope us in to something we won't want to do.'

Once Maggie and Wilf and the fishermen's families had settled in their temporary accommodation, they all gathered in the farmhouse with the farmers and their families. They were given drinks, found seats, and Rick explained exactly what had happened to them and how they had been helped.

'The trouble is,' Rick explained, 'we don't know where Thor will strike next, so we must put in place an alarm system to help each other. This man called Sherebar and his people, have the means to help us, but we can't stand by and do nothing ourselves. Andy and what he's seen, may help them, but we need to talk to them face- to- face. They will be coming here in two days' time.'

Rick rubbed his stubbled jaw and sighed, 'We don't know how, or why we have survived, and others haven't, but perhaps they can explain more to us,' he continued. 'Some of us have been vaccinated with what we thought was a flu vaccine, but now we know it was a vaccine against this virus. We are incredibly lucky and the same may have happened to you, if you had a visit from someone offering the flu vaccine some months ago, before all this happened.' Those round the table nodded their agreement as Rick said. 'We are happy to have you here, and there may be others like us around that we don't know of. We would be grateful for your help with the harvest for the next couple of days if you feel like helping?'

'Anything we can do to help will be fine.' said one of the fishermen. 'The children seem happy having contact with more children. They will help as well. Just tell us what to do.'

'Let's just relax for today.' said Sue joining in the conversation. 'There's not much of the afternoon left once we've fed the animals. If you'd all like to come here I'll do something to eat. The food you've bought with you has been very helpful.'

Over supper of the fish Wilf and the others had bought with them, and chips fried in the oil from the empty fish and chip shop they'd found on their scavenge hunts, it almost felt like normality had returned for a few hours.

CHAPTER TWENTY-NINE

Val and Jenny were talking in the kitchen while David Joshua played on the floor in the hall with Buster and Cassie. There was a knock on the door and Josh came in.

'Can I take David Joshua out?' he asked Val.

'Of course you can if he wants to come,' she said. 'Where's Ginny?' Usually where there's one the other wasn't far behind.

'She's with Pegasus,' said Josh, 'Mums made a picnic so we decided to take a break and thought David Joshua and the dogs would like to come too. Toby is moping as he hasn't seen them much.'

Val got him a jumper and waved them off with a smile. 'A bit of normality in an abnormal world,' she said quietly as they walked out of sight.

David Joshua, who was tall for his age, turned to Josh as he said. 'That wasn't too bad. It's so difficult keeping up the pretence of having a young mind. I wish I could grow my body and be me.'

'Why don't you tell your Mum and Dad?' asked Josh. 'It must be hard keeping your mind closed all the time.'

'I couldn't tell Mum and Dad the truth. They're having enough problems regarding me as it is. Can you imagine how Dad would be if he knew the truth. I'm not sure he would cope, and wouldn't believe I'm his son and not Derebar's,' he said sombrely.

'Are you Derebar's son?' queried Josh. 'You must have something of him in you to be as you are.'

'My DNA will show I am Edwards's son, but Derebar added his essence. From Mum I have abilities of the Sky people. Derebar just unlocked it,' he said.

'Why did you connect with Ginny and me?' asked Josh, 'and who are the Sky people?' he added, confusion filling his young face.

'The Sky people come from the sky, or you could say space. They lived on an Island. You call them tall people, or Atlanteans. Sherebar and Derebar come from them. So do the actual people running Thor. They are mostly good, but when they are bad, they are extremely bad. They want to rule the Universe,' said David Joshua, trying to explain in words that made sense. 'Derebar's spirit comes from the dark side because he died, while Sherebar lived, and always wanted to cause Sherebar pain. He was the unborn child who was chosen to die by his mother, when she couldn't give birth to two live children. Although he seems to have changed a bit, as he wants to keep me safe,' David Joshua said with composure that that belied his age. 'I have this fight of dark and light in me all the time, and it makes me scared. I knew I could trust you Josh, and when Ginny came along, you both being so close, I trusted her too,' he said gravely. 'I think I'd go mad on my own. Thor are looking for me. They think I'm the person from a legend in some old book, and they can use my mind. But for what I don't know.'

'Are you some legend?' asked Josh seriously.

'I don't know,' said David Joshua irritably, with a frown. 'I don't think so, but I won't let them take me. I like it here and being with you two, but they will try, so we need to be ready.' You'll help me, won't you? he pleaded, his eyes watering with unshed tears.

'We're a team, of course we'll help you.' agreed Josh forcibly, his blood boiling at the thought of anyone hurting David Joshua. He'd been named after him Josh, and Edward's dad David, so felt a strong connection to him.

They met Ginny in the field with the dogs and Pegasus, and sat down for a picnic. Buster pushing his nose in as he always did when there was food about. The food was good as usual; Hannah's bread was so moorish especially with home cooked ham. As they ate Josh explained David Joshua's conversation so far, and asked Ginny for her opinion. Buster wandered around with Cassie and Toby, the three of them deciding among themselves that they were going to help too. They always knew the real David Joshua, him being empathic to animals.

'I think you should tell your Mum and Dad, David. You are lucky to have them. I wish I had a Mum or Dad to love me,' said Ginny wistfully. 'I know Hannah and Edward's Dad care for me, so don't get all huffy Josh,' Ginny commented with a grin. 'It's just not quite the same.'

'Well, what do we do about you? Val and Edward will notice sometime.' said Josh, 'and if you're in danger, we all need to be aware. We can't stay in this safe little village for ever.'

'Will you and Ginny be there if I tell them?' asked David Joshua with a tremor in his voice. 'It would be a relief not to have to act all the time, but we might have to tell Grandma Hannah and Grandad too.'

'What about Jenny and Doug? The list is getting longer,' queried Josh.

'I'll tell Mum and Dad first and see what they say,' said David Joshua.

'Why don't we do it now and get it over with?' asked Ginny. Packing up the food left after Buster had helped himself. 'You could take David Joshua home, Josh, and I could get Edward.'

Josh sent Val a message. 'We're bringing David Joshua home, but Ginny and I need a meeting with you and Edward. Can you make sure we can have this without Mrs. Taylor there? Ginny will leave Buster and Toby at the farm. '

'She can take him out' said Val sending the message back through their mind connection. 'What's the matter, is he okay? Her voice sounding worried.

'I'll explain when we arrive, but David Joshua needs to stay with us,' replied Josh.

When they arrived, there was a smell of baking in the air and the side table in the comfortable snug was already laid with strawberry cake, made with produce from the farm, hot rolls, juice, and teacups.

'Come into the snug and tell me what this is about. You're making my stomach churn,' said Val with lines of concern on her face.

'We need to wait for Edward and Ginny,' said Josh eyeing the strawberry cake. 'Can I have some of that while we wait?'

'Me too,' piped up David Joshua.

Val just finished loading their plates when Ginny and Edward came through the door.

'What's this all about?' asked Edward. 'Ginny refused to say, it must be important for you to drag me away from storing the harvest.'

'Mmmm,' said Ginny smelling the hot rolls. 'Can I have one of those before we start? It all looks yummy, and you may want something stronger than that, after this session.' Pointing to the teacups.

'Get on with it then,' said Edward rolling his eyes in irritation.

Ginny looked at Josh and raised her eyebrows. 'I think you should start Josh.'

'Okay David Joshua?' she said looking at him as he nodded. She gave him a thumbs up sign and sat on the floor beside him. Cassie flanked the other side, her head in his lap.

'David Joshua has something to tell you,' stated Josh. 'It will sound fantastical but listen, and don't ask questions until the end. This is hard for him.'

The young boy started talking, Val and Edward looked at him in surprise as his voice had changed and was much more mature than the three and three quarter-year-old he was. 'I am the son of both of you. Please believe me,' he said his voice trembling as he looked at his Dad. 'I have Dad's DNA as well as Mums, but I also have knowledge of her ancestry and abilities, as well as memories of Sherebar and Derebar's people, who I call the Sky people or Sky travellers.' Val and Edward were immobilised with shock, as David Joshua continued.

'Derebar unlocked in me the large part of the brain humans don't use, and that's why I have abilities that you don't realise I have.' Looking at his Mum and Dad with his heart in his eyes. He continued, his voice shaking with the fear of rejection. 'Josh and Ginny as well as Mum, Joe, Sally, and Jenny also have part of this brain store awakening, but not quite to the same extent. Although Josh and Ginny are more advanced, as they had Sherebar's teaching. That's why they knew about me from the start, and I trusted them.' Then with a burst of emotion tears streaming down his cheeks he cried, 'My body doesn't fit my mind, and it is so difficult to live this way.'

Edward looked at his son and despite what he had just heard he saw a distressed nearly four-year-old boy, who he realised he loved completely. It was like a strike of lightning opening his heart. He held out his arms and David Joshua ran into them tears streaking down his face. Edward pulled his son's shaking body close to him, enveloping him in his fiercely protective arms. Val's' eyes filled with tears as she rushed to join them. Her emotions conflicting, she felt protective as well as sad, because she realised her little boy would have a lot to deal with, and Derebar's meddling could cause him so much pain, conflict, and confusion. He had to cope with a child's body, with all the restrictions that meant but an extremely superior mind.

Easing herself out of Edwards arms that still held David Joshua in a close embrace, Val whispered to him. 'We will cope somehow.' As she realised at last that her future was with Edward. She knew she loved him, and they had to nurture this boy, who, and whatever he was. He was their son who needed them. She now had no doubt that Edward loved him as much as she did. She had to stop mourning for a past that would not come back, however much she wished it. This was her life now; she didn't know what the future held and could only hope that it was one they could live in together.

CHAPTER THIRTY

After a call from Joe and Sherebar, a few days later at Rick and Sue's farm. Ginny and Josh arrived with Val and Jenny, and were catching up with everyone.

Sue said. 'We've decided to have a go at sugar extraction from the sugar beet we've been using as animal feed. There is so much hay available now that the beet won't be missed, and sugar is getting harder to find.'

'That's great,' said Jenny who had a sweet tooth. 'The bakery will be pleased. We've managed to source sugar from our store and scavenging but it's getting harder. Val's bought a tray of goodies from the bakers, as we thought we may need a bit of a sugar rush after this meeting. We are lucky with our baker, he's so inventive in the way he uses the ingredients available. He's using honey a lot from our hives. Some of the villagers have begun keeping bees so that helps too.'

'I've left them in the van for the moment,' said Val laughing. 'I didn't think they would last long if I bought them out now. How's it been here with all the new living arrangements?'

'We're managing quite well, thanks to you all, and feel safer. Although we could do with some help preserving and storing. Thank goodness we should have a surplus to put by,' said Sue, as she moved chairs around so they could sit and listen to young Andy when he arrived. 'The extra help has made so much difference especially as we all get on well. There's a deserted orchard just up the road, that Maggie noticed. We could also pick fruit from that, which could add to our store.

'Mmmm, apple pies hopefully?' Ginny said looking at Sue with a grin.

We'll have to see, won't we, depends on if you want to come and help?' replied Sue, returning Ginny's smile.

'We need to wait for Joe, Sally's coming too,' commented Val regarding them all with amusement.' I think I can hear them now. We should get the others together.'

'I'll go,' said Jenny, as she was nearly knocked over by an exuberant Timmy, as he came rushing in, jumping up and down with a big smile on his face. Andy just behind him.

'Joes coming,' said Timmy, jumping up and down with excitement. 'He's taking me, Andy, Josh. and Ginny for a ride in his Black Hawk later, yippee.'

'Ermm,' said his mum with a smile, 'not much hope of you asking me if you can go, first then?'

'Not a hope mum,' answered Timmy, grinning.

As the others filed in eager to hear Andy's story in more detail, Joe and Sally arrived followed by Jenny. 'Are you ready to start, take your time and don't leave anything out. I know you've told some of it before, but the smallest detail might be something important,' said Joe after introducing them all.

Andy, sitting by Maggie, felt reassured by her comforting arm round his shoulder. She gave him a little smile and a nod. He began his story all over again trying not to miss anything out. 'We were all indoors when it began, my Mum, Dad and brother Jason and me. We had stored food and stayed indoors for two weeks as told to. It was boring, but we played games and Dad said it would get better soon, but when we went out Mum freaked out, as there were so many people lying dead in the road and bad smells were coming from some of the houses. She yelled at us to get back indoors. Remembering his Mum and Dad made Andy tremble and Maggie gave him a reassuring squeeze. 'There was no one around, and it was deadly quiet, Mum didn't want me or Jason to go with them,' said Andy with a shudder. The memory still crystal clear. 'We didn't know what was happening, and the people dressed in white suites who were taking bodies away, wouldn't tell us anything. We didn't understand how we were still alive when so many died. '

'Mum and Dad went scavenging most days, and they found a house still with electric, and we moved there with all the food and stuff we had found. It was creepy to think someone had lived there before. The beds were made up, and there was unwashed dishes in the sink. I was sad as I thought the people who lived there must be dead. 'He paused and looked around, feeling a bit more confident, he continued. 'After Mum, Dad and Jason disappeared I was so scared, but kept hoping it would get better or I would find them or that someone would soon come and tell me what I should do.' He sniffed and brushed the back of his hand over his eyes. 'I waited, and waited, but there was no one around. It was very scary. Later I saw a few others and some children in the distance, but they didn't hear me when I shouted, there was no one to help me.'

At this point Andy stopped, tears running down his cheeks, his body shaking in distress. Maggie put her arms round him in a protective embrace and said in a low soothing voice, 'you're doing well love, just say if you want a break, we understand.'

Andy took a deep breath and gradually stopped shaking, wiping away his tears with his sleeve he said in a subdued voice. 'I want to make these people pay for what they've done, and if this helps, I want to tell it.' He continued. 'One day there was a lot of noise from animals howling and barking, I didn't know what to do but I needed food so went out. '

'That's when I met the others, they were scavenging too, but not having much luck, so they came home with me. I thought we would be safer together and was happy to have company. We did quite well at first, but it was getting harder to find food, so when a bus came round, and the people in it said they were from the Government to take us somewhere safe. We said no at first, but some of us wanted to go, I thought of what Dad said about the Government doing something, so we had a vote and decided to go'. He looked at Maggie for reassurance and she nodded for him to continue.

'They showed me pictures and a letter, and it looked okay. I've been sorry about that ever since. They took us to this camp. It was terrible.' He said with a shudder. 'I don't want to talk about it anymore.'

Sally got up and knelt before Andy, taking his hands in hers, saying gently. 'Would you let me look at your memories, it may help us, and won't cause you the stress of explaining more?'

Andy felt the warmth and sympathy flowing through her hands to his, calming his distress. He gave a little nod and closed his eyes almost going into a trance, then slipping into a healing sleep. His body relaxed as Sally explored the information held in his brain.

'Relax,' she said,' you are in a safe place no one can hurt you, and these memories will gradually stop causing you any distress.' She nodded to Maggie to take Andy's hands, and she softly held Andy's head, massaging it slowly, then with one hand covering his nose she gently pulled what looked like a long black insect from his nose, 'do you have a glass jar with a lid?' she asked Sue calmly, 'I need it quickly.'

Sue rushed to the larder, as the others looked on with horror, and bought back one of her preserving jars.

Sally dropped the object in the jar and secured the lid.

'What's that?' asked Josh shuddering, 'it looks gross.'

'It's called an Apis, I don't want anyone mentioning this to Andy, this is serious, it's something we were aware of, but hoped we could sort out before it became a problem. It's not been activated thank goodness, Andy's brain hasn't been effected, so it must have been an accident that it's in Andy.'

'One escaped, and Andy was nearest for it to hide in. The memory was in his subconscious. Joe and I need to get this back to Sherebar as soon as possible, but first, I need to check the other children. The Apis can alter a brain so that the host, in this case Andy, can be controlled.' Sally continued seriously, looking around at the horrified faces. 'Thor want a docile workforce, and although they have the technology to build competent robots, it is easier to use what they have at hand, for example, humans. 'If you don't mind coming with me Maggie, we can make a game of it involving all the children, so that your children aren't frightened,' said Sally looking to the others for agreement, 'Wilf if you could take over from Maggie and sit with Andy. Sue, can you call in all the children for a game in the other room, so it won't seem as if we are singling out Andy's friends?'

'Joe,' said Sally, could you take Ginny, Josh, Timmy, and Andy for a quick ride in the Black Hawk as promised? We could talk about all the information we've gained later.' As she gently woke Andy and left him in Wilf's care.

Maggie and Sally chatting together, walked into the other room. The children already there, looked up expectantly. 'Why don't you sit round in a circle.' said Sally, 'then I'll tell you what we're going to do, we're going to make up a story, and what you have to do is to say a word any word and we will use in the story, 'Maggie would you start.'

'Once upon a time there was' she paused,

Sally stood behind the first child and gently touched their head.

'This is where you say something.' said Sally.

'Chocolate cake,' shouted the child.

'Once upon a time.' said Maggie again. Once Upon a time there was a chocolate cake. It was a big chocolate cake that was squishy in the middle, but it didn't want to be eaten so it…..'

Sally touched the head of the second child, and the child said, 'jumped off the table,'

'Where shall I go now thought the cake?' said Maggie as Sally continued round the circle. The third child said go to the seaside. They followed this process until Sally had been round all the children.

It had been a fun game the children loved it, especially when Sally went into her bag and bought out small bags of jelly sweets she had found on her travels.

'Go out and play now,' Sally said smiling as they went back to join the others.

'Are they okay?' asked Jenny, with trepidation?

'Yes, they're fine,' answered at Sally, 'but we need to do something about Thor's

camp now. It can't wait. Would you all be able to stay together for at least three weeks? I think that would be safer now,' said Sally to the farmers.

'We need to discuss it, but I don't think it would be a problem,' said one of the farmers. We would have to pool the food and perhaps Wilf and the others could go fishing. We could do with a bit of help just now, if you don't mind helping?' he said looking at Wilf and the others.

'What about us?' asked Val with concern. 'There won't be enough of us to take on a whole camp of Thor's.'

'Don't worry,' said Sally soothingly, 'I'll talk to Joe when he gets back, but this is something he needs to talk to his army friends about. Sherebar won't want to alert anyone else to you all for now. Thor don't seem to be taking any special notice of you yet.'

They all looked up as an excited Ginny, Josh, Andy, and Timmy burst through the farmhouse door.

'That was brilliant,' beamed Josh.

'When can we do it again? Can we learn to fly one Joe?' enthused Ginny practically jumping up and down.

Joe laughed and said, 'you both need to talk to Sherebar, it's not up to me, but I think we need to get together for a meeting. We must sort this problem of Thor soon, before the Apis bots become a problem. I'll update you both about these later,' he said to Ginny and Josh, noting their querying looks. 'I would also like you to meet a friend of mine. He's the one I hope will take charge of tackling Thor. He's called The General. He's trustworthy and a good person to have on your side.'

Then there was a buzz from his watch, 'Sal we need to go. Talk to you all later.' he shouted as he drew Sally out of the door, and they ran to the Black Hawk. The craft shot up into the sky and disappeared in a heartbeat.

'What was that all about?' asked a bemused Jenny.

'Not sure, but we had better get going,' said Val as her stomach gurgled and she suddenly felt the need to be home.

CHAPTER THIRTY-ONE

The Black Hawk folded its wings into itself and looked as if it was going to hit the surroundings but instead of that, it just disappeared into the ground and entered a large hanger. Also on the site was Sherebar's hidden headquarters. Sally and Joe climbed out of the Hawk and quickly walked down a well-lit corridor and into a room humming with activity, stark white, with pulsing images of galaxies far away projected on the walls, it was like nothing many had seen on earth before. Only very few humans had seen it, but the privileged few that had, included Joe and Sally. They entered through another entrance into a room much more like a scene on earth. A large table, comfortable chairs, and a counter of fresh bread, cheese, salads, tomatoes, oils, and pastries filled the centre of the room. Luckily for those living here, the facility produced all its own food. The enticing smell of baking permutated the room. Filling their plates, Joe and Sally joined a small group already sitting at the table and Joe proceeded to update his companions on the information Andy had given.

'We need to do something soon,' he said between mouthfuls. 'Finding there are mind controlling Apis at Thor's compound, means we can't delay. These bots are dangerous if they get into a human mind. They could end life on earth as we know it, humans will not be able to think for themselves. When finished here, we should all meet to discuss the next move, as I don't think this is something Val, and the others can manage alone this time.'

Sherebar was already in the meeting room waiting for the others to join him. He was in a contemplative mood and was amazed that a race who only used a fraction of the brain available to them, could have treated their environment, with such disregard over the previous years. But thankfully nature had a habit of regenerating and repairing itself, he had seen glimpses of this already in the re-wilding of empty towns. Sometimes he felt that even those left alive in the world, would be better left to their fate. His figures told him Britain now had only thirty million survivors of their 65 million population. Still a sizeable number to support, as many countries had a significantly smaller percentage of their population still living. These had either been vaccinated or had the genes of the Sherebar's people. Vaccines had been scarce or misused in many countries causing more casualties than even Sherebar had expected. A bad outcome, even he didn't have an answer to everyone's survival. Perhaps it was the way of the universe forcing a realisation on the population, that there was a limit to what the earth would stand.

He sighed and looked up as Sally and Joe entered the room and understood. This pair along with their family were the reason he was still involved. He felt a strong attachment to this small group. They would fight for what they believed in, and he hoped with his help they would win. Four others of his race also joined them in the command room and sat down. The mood was sombre, as if there was a dark cloud hanging over the room.

'How should we handle this?' asked Joe as he looked around and sat down. 'Val and the others don't have the manpower to cope with the Apis situation even with Josh, Ginny, and the other teenagers. We need to talk to The General soon. What do you think? The Apis mean we can't delay. They need to be destroyed.'

'We have to try and keep Val and the others away from this,' agreed Sally with concern, 'I don't think we should draw attention to them now, as we may need their abilities for the final battle that I'm sure will come. It will be a miracle if we can keep Josh and Ginny away from this though, their powers are too intuitive. They will know we're planning something.'

One of the other four said 'I agree, can we talk to the General now? We need to start making plans immediately.'

He's already on his way 'commented Sherebar with a smile. 'As soon as I heard the location of the Apis I spoke to him. We need to keep in mind that there are some of our race involved in Thor. That's why the Apis has been hidden so well. If it hadn't been for Andy, we may not have found out about the Apis until it was too late.'

There was a knock on the door and Marika entered with a tray of enticing little sandwiches and a steaming drink. 'I thought you might like this while you wait for The General. Even we like coffee and food to lighten tense situations,' she said calmly. Her presence sending waves of positivity around the room. Joe got up and gave her a hug, telling the others how she was one of the special people in his life. As it was Marika who had arranged his magical wedding to Sally.

'Sit down Marika, and join us,' said Sherebar, 'we could

do with your input on how we manage this situation. We can't afford to fail. If the Apis are released there will not be much we can do, and this planet will be doomed, or rather the people on it will.'

'Don't they deserve it?' One of those round the table grimly asked Sherebar,

Sherebar shrugged his shoulders and sighed. 'Some of those left do, but there are many who don't. I am committed to help,' he said with sudden steel in his voice. 'Although I also have had doubts. Please confirm if you are still willing to do this.'

There was a pause, and Joe and Sally looked at each other with concern. It was serious if Sherebar had doubts of his own race helping them.

Then one of the group said, 'I'm with you. I like this planet. We came to help and it's why we are here, it's what we must do.' Then one by one they all agreed, including Marika.

CHAPTER THIRTY-TWO

Ginny didn't know how to explain how she was feeling, she just knew she had to get away, even from Josh. She needed some space. She ran to the field calling to Pegasus as she went. He looked up neighed and galloped towards her. She jumped on his back with all the grace of a ballet dancer, although she was tall with an athletes build, and leant forward to give him a hug. Holding onto his mane, no reigns, or saddle, she was as at one with her horse. They flew over hedges and ditches into the open farmland. At first it was well cultivated, looked after with care by the villagers as well as Edward, Hannah, her partner, Edwards Dad, and their workers, but the further they went the wilder it became. She felt the exhilaration of the speed, the joy of being with Pegasus and the wind blowing through her hair.

They entered a wood that still had pathways trodden by the animals who had made it their home, the sun shone through the leaves making lacy patterns on the ground. Ginny slid from Pegasus's back and he followed her to a stream that bubbled down a rocky outcrop forming a pool that both Pegasus and she drank from. The smell from wild-flowers, berries, and herbs, filled the air. Birds called and a Sparrow Hawk hovered above. Sitting on the bank, Pegasus quietly grazing beside her she thought back over the last two years. Where would she have been if she hadn't met Sherebar at school? What would have happened to her brother and sister? She knew they wouldn't have been in a good place, and she should be grateful, but she wanted more. Josh did too. Val had her hands full keeping the village going. It was a big responsibility, but Ginny felt Val was restless too.

They worked as a team her and Josh with Jenny, and the others. This is when she felt most alive. She felt strongly that she and Josh at least, should be involved in whatever scheme Sherebar had for rescuing the other captive children. If they didn't include them, she knew they would go anyway. They just had to be there. Feeling a presence, she looked up to see Josh and three dogs approaching.

'What are you doing here?' she asked abruptly, in a not too friendly voice. 'I came for a bit of space.'

'I, or rather the dogs, just followed your scent, you were sending out angry signals and I wanted to know why,' replied Josh reasonably. 'I Just wished you'd slowed down a little, even the dogs are a bit out of breath.'

~

'A bit out of breath', said Buster to himself panting hard, don't they realise we're getting older, there's no way we can keep up with Pegasus.' Then thinking of his stomach as usual his tongue hanging out, he nudged Cassie, 'I hope there's something for us in the packed lunch I know Josh has.' It was a happy thought. Cassie nudged Buster back and sat down sighing with pleasure at the rest after the long run, Buster knew Cassie understood what he was saying as they had always talked to each other by reading each other's minds since they were puppies. Buster always happy if his stomach was filled looked hopefully at Josh who was ignoring him.

'Alright, sit down we have something to discuss.' said Ginny with resignation giving the dogs a hug. Buster and Cassie moved and sat down beside them and looked at them both as if to say, we want to be involved too. 'There's so much noise about,' Ginny continued. 'I'm wondering if it's from us or Thor. If I've noticed it, others will have too. I'm feeling trapped in something, but don't know what or how to get out of it. I just needed some thinking space.'

'Aren't you happy with us?' responded Josh. 'I can't imagine you not being around. You're my best friend, and Mum, and my David, love you too. Bel and Tip are happy with us and have started calling them, Mum, and Dad, Is that a problem?' queried Josh with concern.

'No that's not a problem, said Ginny thoughtfully. I'm happy they've settled so well, but I was used to making all my own decisions and looking out for them. The last two years have been a big adjustment. I'm grateful to your Mum, Val, and the others for all they've done, but I need to make my own decisions now. I want to help free those children,' answered Ginny forcefully, with a sideways glance at Josh, because she knew full well, he thought the same on this.

'Okay then,' said Josh with a grin of relief. 'What do we do about it?'

He sat down beside her, bringing out the food he had the foresight to grab as he left. His mum always had ready packed food in the fridge, knowing some persons or other, namely Josh and or Ginny were always rushing off somewhere. The dogs sat round hoping there would be something in the backpack for them too. Luckily as usual Hannah had packed their favourite sausages.

'I love Hannah,' sighed Buster.

'Let's decide how we get to Sherebar without causing a fuss and a search party. We can't just call him the others will know if we do. It's a bit complicated to send all we want to say in mind talk too, but we could try,' said Ginny as she grabbed a sandwich and grinned at Josh. Her mood lightening at the thought of action.

Back at the Village, Val was at her desk when Edward arrived. 'Want a break,' he asked, 'let's walk by the river, I saw Ginny heading out with Pegasus, they were flying along. That girl certainly has a way with horses. '

'Josh was going somewhere with the dogs too,' said Val with a smile. 'Hannah said the packed lunches had gone from the fridge. I wonder what they're planning now.'

'I'm sure we'll find out soon enough.' countered. Edward with a grin. 'They certainly add spice to life, even if they make it than more complicated than we would like. '

As they walked by the river Val felt more peaceful than she had for a long while. She'd accepted nothing could ever be the same again, and that her relationship with Edward was gradually repairing itself. She wasn't naive enough to not understand that there would be tough times ahead, but knew she had to take whatever uptimes there were. She took Edward's hand, always so warm and comforting and a small spark of hope began to grow in her mind.

'What do you think we should do about the children trapped in the Thor compound? Ginny and Josh will be planning something you can be sure of that,' asked Edward, squeezing her hand and pulling her close.

Suddenly Val broke away running back towards the farm. 'Edward run.'

'What's the matter?' said Edward in alarm.

'They're trying to take David Joshua,' Val cried in desperation. 'I don't think we'll be in time. He's fighting to stay awake, but they've injected him with something and he's struggling.'

They both arrived at the Home Farm panting and out of breath just as a Hawk like plane shot into the air and disappeared.

Val fell to the ground sobbing, her shoulders shaking. Her baby, he might have an incredible brain, but he was her little boy and would want his mum, she wanted to scream, her stomach churning, but suddenly she changed. She turned to Edward who was grey and shaking himself, and said, 'we must call Sherebar.'

'And although I don't like the idea.' said Edward with a sigh. 'We need to ask him to contact Derebar. We need all the help we can get.' He continued as he gently wiped her tears.

Val knew what that would cost him to ask Derebar for anything, considering what he had put Edward through in the past.

After a fraught call to Sherebar, Val contacted Jenni, Doug, Ginny, and Josh. When they all arrived at the same time they were confronted with a now distraught, barely coherent, Edward and Val.

'Whatever's happened,' asked Jenny with concern as she rushed to put her arms round Val. 'Val, Edward, what's happened, is David Joshua okay?'

Edward shook his head and said. 'They've taken David Joshua,'

'Who's taken him?' asked Doug, knowing from the scene before him that it was something serious.

'We don't know,' said Val trying to stop herself panicking, 'but think it must be Thor,' her body still shaking from the shock. 'I've contacted Sherebar, but we need to do something ourselves. I can't sit here and do nothing.'

'Have you any idea where they've taken him?' asked Jenny stroking Val's hair

'No,' said Val, 'but Sherebar is searching for him. We need to get to his facility as soon as possible.'

'That's a fair way to go,' said Doug. 'What if they've taken him to the camp where they were holding Andy? We're nearer to that, than we are to Sherebar. I know Joe's got at least one Hawk, but we may be able to get to Andy's compound quicker.'

'I think we should go in now,' said Ginny forcefully, thinking of how she would feel if it was Tip or Bel.

'I agree,' said Josh with conviction, 'David Joshua's a clever boy he'll hold them off as long as possible, but he's still only young and we're not sure of all his abilities yet.'

'We need to hear from Sherebar first,' said Doug, with the voice of reason, he may have more of an idea where he is. We don't want to go in there not being fully prepared or go to the wrong place. We know there are some of Sherebar's race there, they can read minds remember, so we must be careful. We don't want to put David Joshua in more danger than he's already in.'

'I can't sit here and do nothing,' said Val with agitation,' we need to do something now!'

'I agree,' said Doug, in a soothing voice, 'but we ought to look at what we have here, that will help us in any fight we're going to have. Are any of the teenagers or villagers strong enough to help us? If the kidnapped children are there, we can't leave them behind. So, we need to organise transport and a place of safety to take them.'

Jenny nodded her agreement. Doug knew that her heart ached for Val and Edward. He also understood the need Val and Edward had for action, but if they didn't plan, they may fail, and Jenny's mischievous nephew could pay the price.

'Get the villagers together now, and we'll see who can drive the vans and make sure they are ready to go at a moment's notice. We may need medical supplies, and someone to go in the vans with the children if we find them.' Doug continued with authority, 'they'll be traumatised and frightened. Any volunteers will also need directions to the Thor camp and be warned not to approach too near until called. Hannah and David need to take over here,' said Doug calmly. Knowing that Edward wasn't the right state to plan anything just now.

'Josh, Ginny, no doing your own thing. If you come, you're part of a team.' Doug warned as they arrived. 'Go and sort the dart guns, and anything else that you think will be useful.'

'Joe has just sent a message,' said Jenny with relief. 'David Joshua is at the same camp that kept Andy, and they are just discussing tactics; he says to remember some have Sherebar's ability so keep your minds blocked. For this reason, plans will be released in stages.'

'I can't just sit here doing nothing,' cried Val again in despair, wringing her hands and pacing back and forward.

'We're not doing nothing Val.' Doug explained gently. 'Edward, can you sort the transport. Coaches would be better than vans if we can find them. Jenny, you take Val and talk to the villagers. Josh, Ginny, you know what you must do. I'll talk to Hannah, David, Ma, and Dr Foster. Meet in an hour at the village hall. Sherebar should have a plan by then.'

'Well, you sorted that very efficiently,' said Jenny with a wry smile.

'Someone had to,' countered Doug gently taking her hand. 'We can't just charge in, and you need to be careful. You've given me enough shocks in the past to turn my hair grey. I would rather not have any more.'

Jenny gave a little shudder. Doug had nearly died testing the vaccine on himself. He had been there when she had been kidnapped before the virus struck. They were bonded together by experiences, as well as love.

'Here we go again,' she said a tear in her eyes. 'Please let David Joshua be okay,' she prayed, to a God she no longer believed in.

Cassie was licking the tears from Val's face and Buster followed Jenny out.

'You're not coming with us Buster; you must stay with Hannah and Edward's Dad.' said Jenny.

Buster nodded, but Jenny knowing her dog, guessed that he and Cassie had already decided they were going with Josh and Ginny.

CHAPTER THIRTY-THREE

David Joshua hadn't realised what was happening until it was too late, but he understood if he were to help himself, he would have to send a message quickly before the drug they had given him worked. He also blocked his mind so that no one could read it or understand the true extent of his abilities.

The two people in the craft were talking among themselves while keeping an eye on the comatose child. One said, 'that wasn't too hard, was it? Luckily the parents weren't around. We may have had a bit of a struggle if they had been there. The woman looking after him wasn't a problem at all,'

'Have you tried looking into his brain?' the other asked.

'I tried but it's blocked, but I'm sure one of the others will be able to overcome his defences.'

'Is he one of us?' asked the first one

'I'm not sure,' said the second, 'but he must be something special for the boss to take these risks.'

The craft landed. The limp child was gently carried into a room with a large chair, bed, and other equipment. Another man entered the room. He was tall, standing straight with long slender hands and an aquiline face. Dressed as a hospital doctor, in a white coat and trousers, he looked at the child and said, 'he will be sleeping a while, but I want someone to stay with him. Let me know the minute he wakes.'

As David Joshua woke up, he took in his surroundings noted the bareness of the room and the equipment on the adjoining wall. Careful to make sure that no one realised he was conscious, he sent his location and a picture of the room to Sherebar. Then making sure he had suitable blocks on his mind he gradually opened his eyes.

The man by the bed smiled at him and offered him a drink of juice. David Joshua refused and stared at the man until he had to look away. The man lowered his eyes and pressed a button to call the man, dressed as a doctor, back.

'Well, David Joshua,' the doctor said as he arrived. 'It's good to meet you at last. I hope you enjoy your stay with us. We are going to get on very well I think and as you're an intelligent boy, you will soon realise that we can offer you a better way of living, where you will not have to hide your intelligence and are appreciated.'

David Joshua smiled to himself, and thought, you have no idea. He felt them trying to look in his mind and looked at them innocently as if he didn't realise what they were doing.

'I think you should remove the block on your mind now, don't you young man?' the doctor asked with a grimace. 'Doing that will just cause problems and we will breakdown your defences in the end. It would be much simpler if you co-operated. There's no point in acting dumb, As I and others, know what you're capable of and there are ways of making you talk to us.'

'I'll give you time to think about it. Don't take too long, we'll be moving out by the end of the week and it's up to you if it's pleasant or not.' He smiled as he left the room

'Derebar where are you?' David Joshua whispered to himself. 'Why are you never around when you're needed?'

He could see that there were cameras and sensors in the room and felt that there was a watch on this mind. He could get round that, but there was not much time. As clever and powerful as he was, he knew there was not much chance of breaking out of this room without help. He still had the body of a child to contend with. The little boy in him just wanted his Mum and Dad. He knew they would be trying to find him. He just hoped they would be in time.

CHAPTER THIRTY-FOUR

The village alert system was working. Many of the villagers had answered the distress call. Edward explained that David Joshua had been kidnapped, although most had already heard on the village grapevine.

'We haven't got much time,' said Edward, his voice still shaky with emotion.' I don't know if any of you will be willing to help us rescue David Joshua and the other children. It could be dangerous. These kidnappers are not people to take on lightly. There is no shame in not wanting to help,' he said seriously. 'Val and I quite understand, but we must decide what to do quickly. Doug will now explain what we need.' With that Edward went to find Val and Jenny. They needed to talk to Sherebar.

By now, most of the villagers now knew how lucky they had been to live in this village. They hadn't suffered as much as some, like the farm and Lily's family. They had all heard the stories. The village had food, water, work, and better security than others. They may have moaned in the beginning, but seeing what had happened to the rest of the country their life had been comparatively comfortable. Now time to do their bit. They gathered round in groups, a bit on edge, just wanting to get on with whatever Doug asked of them.

As Doug spent a bit of time talking to the volunteers and setting their tasks, an urgent message came through from Jenny.

'Come now,' she said, her voice thick with emotion. 'We need to act quickly.'

'Sorry I have to go,' he said to the villages as he ended the conversation. 'I must leave but keep yourselves ready. We will be moving at short notice.'

Running to the control room he arrived the same time as Josh, Ginny, and the dogs. Rubbing Busters head he said, 'what are you two doing here?'

Buster looked at Cassie their heads down not looking Doug. They were going to stick to Josh and Ginny like glue, as they already had an idea what Josh and Ginny were planning. There was no chance, they would be left behind. Dooley, Josh's pet rat had already been given her task. She'd been invaluable when helping Josh in the past. Rats had a bad press but were intelligent and she was able to get into places others couldn't. Their teeth could chew through most things. Disabling electronics her speciality.

~

They all sat round the screen as Sherebar appeared. 'I have talked to The General,' he said, 'he's one of us. You can trust him. We must act within the three days I calculate it will take, before they can move the Apis. Joe will oversee neutralising them,' he said his voice conveying how serious he felt the need for quick action was. 'That's imperative, as if they are released the situation will take a dangerous turn. They can enter the human brain via the nose or ears and are hard to detect. This enables Thor to control the victims. I know you are aware of their danger, as you saw the inactivated one Sally took from Andy.' He looked at Josh and Ginny, knowing they were itching to get going.

'Josh and Ginny, I want you to focus on getting the children out. I have arranged for coaches to meet you at a place you will be informed of when they are nearby. These are to pick up any captives and children freed. We must keep communication to a minimum as we don't want unexpected intrusion into the driver's minds. There aren't many of my race at this compound, but as they have David Joshua security may be increased.'

'Do you know how he is?' agonised Val. 'He's not able to contact me. I've tried and he's blocked.'

Doug put a comforting arm around her. 'We're going to get him back,' he said. 'Or die trying', he added softly, for his ears only.

Doug asked Sherebar. 'Is there anything Edward and I can do to protect ourselves? We don't have the other's powers, and I wouldn't want a stray thought to jeopardise the operation.'

'Two helmets will be with you in two hours. They are tight fitting with communicators. All The General's troops will have them too but keep communication to a minimum.'

'Be ready to go when contacted. Stay two miles away from the compound until told otherwise.' With that Sherebar abruptly disappeared.

Jenny turned to Doug and slipped her hand in his. 'This wasn't what you signed up for when we met, was it?' she asked.

'No,' he said tightening the grip on her hand, 'life is

certainly more eventful around you. But I don't regret it. Don't ever think that,' as he whispered, 'I love you.'

'Break it up you two.' Commented Ginny. 'We've got to get everything ready. Come on Josh, Buster, Cassie, let's go. '

'You're not thinking of taking the dogs, are you?', asked Jenny with concern.

'There's no way we would get away without them,' said Josh. 'Just try it.'

'They'll be in the way. Buster,' warned Jenny.

'Cassie stay,' said Val.

'We won't be in the way,' grumped, Buster to Cassie. Communicating through their minds as they had done all their lives.

'Don't worry.' replied Cassie, 'they'll be so busy they won't notice we're gone until it's too late.'

With that, the two large white dogs laid down and pretended to sleep. Creeping out to follow Ginny and Josh when the others were occupied.

CHAPTER THIRTY-FIVE

The transport was ready to go, and the coach drivers had been given their meeting point. Doug and Edward's helmets arrived and caused a bit of light relief as they struggled to put them on. All were in dark protective clothing including those villagers helping. There was a lot of tension in the air. No one knew quite what to expect, even Val, Jenny, Doug, and Edward were apprehensive. They had more of an idea than the others of what they would face, and that didn't help much.

Val was so agitated, she just wanted to get going. Her baby was at risk. Her stomach was churning. She hated being out of touch with him for so long. Edward gave her arm a squeeze of reassurance although he admitted to himself, he felt bad too.

'Where's Ginny and Josh?' asked Jenny suddenly. 'They should be here by now.'

They're a law unto themselves, those two,' agreed Edward.

'We can't wait for them, said Val, 'Sherebar's just sent our directions. You can be sure they'll find their way somehow. I just wish they would do as they're told sometimes.'

~

Ginny and Josh had decided to make their own way to the compound, Joe had sent comprehensive directions, and told them not try to join Sherebar's team led by the General. They needed to get the children out first. They had already gone to see Wilf and he was willing to take them as far as Harwich in his boat.

Josh sent Val a message, knowing it was far too late for her to stop them, to say he and Ginny had been in touch with Sherebar. Making sure they were not seen, they were stealthily approaching the compound from a different angle to Val's group. This was to be sure they were at the side of the compound near the large gates. Where the children's accommodation was most likely to be situated, according to Andy's recollection. If Andy's information of the children's location was correct it would help speed up evacuation. Lewis and Ella would also be with them soon, as well as the dogs. They had head gear for them, and coats for the dogs, Sherebar having sent theirs separately, knowing full well, how they would operate. The General's team would see them in about two hours.

'Typical,' said Val to herself when she received the message. But she knew she had to just trust them, as in some areas, together they were more powerful than her and Jenny.

CHAPTER THIRTY-SIX

'You two seem to be joined at the hip,' observed Ginny as Lewis and Ella came over to join them.

'You can talk,' said Lewis. 'What about you and Josh?'

Ginny looked at Josh quizzically.' I suppose you're right,' agreed Ginny. 'We just clicked. It was strange being here at first, and Josh helped a lot.'

'You wouldn't have had so much fun without me,' said Josh with a grin, 'and it's more interesting with you around. Although you're quite prickly sometimes.'

'Me prickly? You would be too if you'd had to live my life before I came here,' retorted Ginny.

'Did you have to leave anyone behind when you came here?' Ginny asked Lewis with interest.

'No,' he said sadly. 'I only had a Mum. Never knew my Dad. Mum died when I was sixteen. By chance I became an apprentice at the wind farm, I liked working there, and was lucky Ella's Dad took me with him. It's something I really appreciate now. It's good being part of this team, it's more adventurous than I could ever have dreamed of. Despite all the problems, it has its positive side. It was so scary when Ella, her Mum, and Dad were kidnapped, but I'm so much better off here.'

'That was so frightening.' agreed Ella. 'It still gives me nightmares thinking of what could have happened, that's why I want to help destroy Thor. If it weren't for my brother Alistair wanting to bring us here, I don't know what would have become of us.' She shivered as the thought of what might have happened if they hadn't been rescued. It made her feel physically sick. The threats the man made still so clear in her mind.

'Are you sure you want to come with us?' asked Ginny, having no illusions as to how dangerous the next few hours could be.

'Yes', said Lewis and Ella in unison. 'We make a good team and have more power together.'

'We better get going then.' said Josh 'Wilf will be meeting us at the boat,'

'Aren't we going with the others?' asked Lewis.

'What do you think?' said Josh. 'Buster and Cassie want to come with us, and Val and Jenny would stop that. They're so good with children and we may need their help. Buster was brilliant when I was younger and had to escape from a holiday park.'

'Won't it be dangerous for them?' asked Ella.

'Buster's been with me in more dangerous situations. They know when to act or disappear. Val and Jenny are just a bit more anxious about them now, as they are both getting older. However they're fitter than they realise. We need to meet Wilf. Get in, we must get going.' Josh said pointing to the waiting van.

'Remember it would be a good idea to get there in one piece,' said Ginny knowing Josh's love of speed.

Josh grinned at her, 'you can talk,' he said.

The countryside was looking better as they sped along the road. The farm where their friends lived, had expanded with the help of a few more survivors. These had found themselves near the farm, when looking for a place to stay away from abandoned towns. It was becoming quite a big community and was working well.

Wilf was waiting for them at the harbour, they loaded their equipment and the dogs' special coats into the boat and Wilf cast off. The water was still and there was only a slight breeze. 'Just hope it stays like this,' said Wilf indicating the calm sea. 'How will you get from the drop off point, to the meeting point?' he asked. He knew these young people were resourceful but was still concerned. He liked them and wanted them to be safe.

'We'd already looked for transport, as we were sure once we knew David Joshua had been kidnapped, there would be a rescue mission, and we wanted to be ready,' said Josh. 'But Joe said there would be some transport waiting so not to worry. Thor don't monitor the sea or river area, according to Joe.' 'If there is a problem with the General's troop, we still have another chance to get David Joshua out.'

'Do you want me to wait for you?' enquired Wilf.

'Yes', said Ginny, 'but it may be late before we get back. Don't put yourself at risk, your children need you. We'll find our own way back if you're not here.'

Wilf thought himself lucky to have met the farmers, the villagers, and these young people. It gave him hope that there was a future for them all, if only they could contain Thor. Not in his wildest dreams would he have expected to meet a group like this four. They all worked as a team. There were a few arguments as you would expect with some of the strong characters involved.

He'd loved his old life, and missed his son and grandchildren, whom he still hadn't heard from, but surprisingly he was enjoying the life he was now leading. What a blockbuster this would make. Perhaps he should write a script to tell future generations, he mused, as the boat sailed quickly to its destination. The weather was with them and if it hadn't been such a dangerous mission, it would be a lovely day to go sailing. Wilf thought he might try fishing while he waited. They had to stay out of sight until dusk and needed to make sure they weren't seen by Thor before then. He'd never seen any other fishermen than those he knew about, but perhaps there were some more out there. He'd have to go looking one day.

It took them a bit longer than they expected due to the currents, to reach the harbour. Everywhere was deserted. The boats untended, cranes rusting and there was an air of melancholy about the place, not a soul about. He saw a dog howling in the distance and a fox with its cubs sniffing around for its evening meal. *What a sad fate for what once was a busy port with tankers from all over the world,* thought Wilf. He expertly docked his boat and the small group disembarked. Including the dogs.

'I think it would be safer for you to wait out at sea,' said Josh. 'Here's the communicator. I will contact you on it when we are ready or if we decide to go back another way.'

Wilf watched as they put the dogs in their camouflage suits and Lewis and Ella donned on the head gear. Wilf's heart felt heavy as he didn't know if he would ever see them all again.

CHAPTER THIRTY-SEVEN

They skirted round the port to an abandoned business park. The small manufacturers here quiet, and most empty. Windows were broken and dirty, weeds growing through concrete, no longer a bustling hub of activity, except for two buildings that looked as if they were still in use.

Josh strode towards them and opened one of the large doors. Inside was a smiling Mike, the engineer, son in law of Mrs Upton from the village.

'See you made it then,' he said, 'wish it was under better circumstances,'

'What are you doing here?' queried Ginny surprised and a bit annoyed. 'Why did you keep it a secret Josh?'

'I didn't know until this morning and wanted it to be a surprise.'

'You'd better explain Mike,' said Josh.

'When Sherebar found out that I was an engineer who had been working on these vehicles, he suggested that I joined some of his team working with the developers of a similar vehicle. There were only prototypes before the virus hit. Unfortunately, not many of my workmates survived. Those that did, were quickly introduced to Sherebar's people and are working on other projects now.'

'These vehicles are energy efficient, revolutionary, and robust. Many of the vehicles laying around now are polluting. Luckily, their components can be recycled into other more useful goods. We are stockpiling what we can for future use.' Mike explained. 'This is also how Thor are finding materials to reuse for other projects, with so many mines shut down. The units used to manufacture these new vans, cars, and trucks are easy to dismantle and rebuild. They don't take up much room and can be completely automated.' Mike said, with pride at the achievement.

'Although the electric trucks and cars we use now are good, their battery life is limited. New batteries of the right size will be hard to manufacture due to lack of the right material. These new vehicles take minuscule batteries, and we have a large store of them. Sherebar having the foresight to produce these in advance. Thankfully they also last for years when fully charged.' He paused, looking at these young people and admiring their bravery.

'How is it Thor doesn't know about these?' interrupted Lewis with interest.

'They were so secret that no one in the workforce knew what the finished product would be, until just before the virus. Then there was so much else to worry about no one found out.' said Mike. 'The factories were small and movable and with very few workers, that they were below the radar of everyone but the developers, who had been vaccinated by Sherebar.'

'It was a complete fluke the developers had come to Sherebar's notice. Unfortunately, he was not able to save all the staff. I hope many survived. I was lucky to have found your village, so I was vaccinated in time,' Mike said clasping his hands to stop them shaking, as he remembered all those lost. 'When Sherebar came to see Val, she mentioned that I had been an engineer, he talked to me, and it all went from there. This small business park was a good place to hide what I was doing.'

'How is it no one read your mind?' asked Ella wondering if he knew about the extra abilities some of them had. 'Does Molly know what you do?'

'It was lucky no one tried,' said Mike to answer Ella's question about mind reading. 'Sherebar warned me about the risk, I've protection now. Molly doesn't know anything about the prototype, it's too dangerous. She's used to me disappearing for months on end. I'm sorry but you will all have to have this location wiped from your minds when you next see Sherebar.' Realising they may not be too happy with that, he led them through a door to a large room which housed a black van.

'Wow,' said Josh, 'that looks sleek.' The front curved, clean lines, and no visible wheels. 'How do we get to use it when it's so secret?'

'It has several features we need to test in various scenarios. Sherebar knew you would learn its controls quickly. There are many of them. We need to go through those controls now, as there's not much time,' answered Mike

'It will self-destruct if necessary, and if you can't use it to return, it will allow Edward to control it as it will recognise his DNA. He's the only other person in the village to know about the continuation of the project. Otherwise, it can return automatically, and will act if followed.

'What's it called?' enquired Ginny

'Electair,' answered Mike. 'It's powered by air and electric, I'll show you.'

Mike touched the side of the van and it opened to show

soft lighting, seats a large cargo area at the back, and a row of dials in front.

'It can run on air, and this is mostly the way to use it. You don't always need the wheels for this, and it saves battery power, but if you need a fast getaway press for full power and the wheels will appear. Use these for landing if you use air over fields.'

It's completely silent and has a camouflage option which you need to use today.' Explained Mike. He made sure they all understood the commands and dials, and gave them a quick run, around the local area.

'Don't worry,' he said seeing Ella's concerned face. 'No one can see us.' It's programmed for the compound. Good luck and keep safe.' He jumped out of the van and watched as the small group slowly left the shed. Good luck to them he thought, they were brave and resourceful but so young. Should they be trusted with this project? He wasn't sure, but Sherebar wouldn't have sent them to him if he'd had any doubts.

CHAPTER THIRTY-EIGHT

They stopped just over a mile from the compound, and Josh sent a coded message to Edward letting him know where they were, and the location of the transport. It was getting dark when they reached the gates nearest to the children's accommodation. The dogs were subdued and following closely behind.

The security system had been cleverly deactivated by Dooley, Josh's pet rat and her friends, and it wouldn't be noticed by the control for at least another hour, with luck. Security round the children was not a priority for Thor, as all their sheds were now bolted from the outside at night. Something Dooley had been able to warn Josh about.

Ginny used her lock picking skills to unlock the gate, and they were in.

'We need to take out the guards,' whispered Ginny. 'Joe said that according to his surveillance information there are two in this area, but they only check every hour, we have ten minutes before the next one.'

They melted into the shadows when suddenly Buster

gave a low growl, as two men dressed in a dark uniform and chatting amiably came round the corner.

'What's that?' said one.

'Probably a fox,' said the other. 'Quite a few around here. Dogs aren't allowed in this part of the compound. '

Just then simultaneous darts hit them in the chest, and they dropped to the ground like a stone. Pulling them into the shadows Josh and the others began unbolting the doors.

~

Beth was sitting on her thin mattress a tear rolling down her cheek. The room was bare just floor-boards, their beds, a basin, and two toilets they had to clean themselves. *They were the rubbish* girls *and boys* she thought, spending their days sorting through piles of rubbish every day. She didn't know that resources were scarce, and this was a cheap way to recycle. The children didn't cost much and were expendable.

Beth wasn't sure where the rubbish came from, or where it went when it was sorted. It was put on a conveyor belt and the children had to sort the glass bottles, plastic, and metal, into bins behind them. It was dirty and sometimes smelly. She and the others had to stand for hours at a time, too frightened to stop.

Like Andy's group who fitted metal bits together, they didn't dare complain and the children were so tired that some fainted and weren't seen again. The break for food was only 30 minutes and was usually something disgusting and taken with a handful of pills. If any of them refused to take them, they were beaten. They soon learned to do as they were told.

Can no one help us she thought, *why don't they care? Does anyone know we are here?* She didn't know if her parents were dead or alive, and like the others had seen so many distressing scenes that she had to block them from her mind. Then she heard a noise at the door. Her heart nearly stopped with fear. She started to shake, and held her breath, as the door opened and a tall girl dressed in dark clothing, and distinctive red hair entered. She had her hand to her lips to warm them to keep quiet, and a boy similarly clothed followed with a large dog who was also wearing a dark covering.

'Wake the others but tell them to be quiet, that's important, we're going to get you out of here, but we don't have much time,' said the girl quietly.

Beth looked at her in amazement and for a moment didn't know what to do. Then a flicker of hope rose in her heart, and she hurriedly woke the others up.

'Be quiet,' she said putting her hand to her lips. 'There's someone here to help us.'

'This is Buster,' said the boy pointing to the large dog, as he watched the sad little group wake up. 'Follow Buster,' he said. 'He will take you to help and safety, but you must be incredibly quiet, don't talk. Do you understand?'

The children looked traumatised and exhausted but nodded agreement, and did as they were told,

'How do we know we can trust you?' said Beth quietly, her body still trembling with fear.

Ginny sent the children some calming waves and the small group felt better. Including Beth

'Buster', said Josh pointing to the dog. 'He will lead you out of here. 'Don't lose sight of him. It's not far to help and we must go and help others now,' said Josh quietly.

Buster led the children the short way to the open gate without incident, taking care that he didn't lose any. Keeping to the shadows and away from windows. Cassie met him at the gate and between them they managed to deliver all the children safely to those waiting, Beth gave both dogs a hug, marvelling that she hadn't been frightened of two large dogs. She was just wondering why the alarm hadn't gone off, when a woman beckoned them, and they were taken to a coach already loaded with several children. More arrived, and the coach soon filled up and being electric powered, quietly left the compound. Beth felt she should be scared, but for some reason she trusted these people to help her.

There were two women and a man inside the coach. The woman said, 'my name is Lisa, and this is Sam, pointing to the other woman, and Ira, (a tall thin man with long dark hair), is going to come round with drinks and food as I expect you are hungry and thirsty. We are taking you somewhere safe and will find you a place to live soon, so you're not frightened all the time.'

'Why should we believe you anymore than those that kidnapped us?' asked one of the older children. Feeling braver and more hopeful than he'd felt for a long time.

'We can't make you trust us.' agreed Ira as he handed out drinks and food. 'All we can do is show you that we mean what we say. Have a drink, something to eat and try and sleep, we will be somewhere safe in about two hours.'

As they drove silently through the deserted countryside the children tired with exhaustion and fear started to fall asleep. The driver, thankful that there was no one pursuing them turned the lights off, and the coach steadily followed the pre-programmed route. The driver hoped the other coaches hadn't had any problems either.

They eventually arrived at a large building that was once a boarding school purposely remodelled for this eventuality, as many orphaned children had been foreseen by Sherebar. The building was lit up with several lights and there were many people with blankets and hot drinks standing by. The children were eventually taken to a room already filled with lots of children of all ages.

On a stage stood a tall commanding woman in colourful clothes. She said in a calming voice. 'My name is Marika, and I will make sure you are looked after, there is no need to be frightened anymore. I know it will be difficult for you to trust us, but we can talk more in the morning when you have slept and had breakfast. We want to hear your stories.'

'You will be taken to bedrooms where you can sleep in safety and comfort, and tomorrow, we will talk more about how we can help you and keep you safe.' Her voice was such that some, but not all, of the children were reassured.

In small groups and making sure that those that knew each other were kept together, they were taken to bedrooms with six beds a room, containing duvets and warm blankets. The children were also shown sparkling clean wet rooms and toilets, where they could have the privacy to have a shower before they slept. There were comfy bed clothes in various sizes hanging on the wall.

Some of the children were so traumatised they couldn't sleep, but calming music was played through a speaker lulling them eventually into a fitful sleep. Teddy bears were on every bed, adding comfort, and a sense that things may be getting better, began to be felt by the children. Dimmed lights were left on to add to the sense of security.

Sherebar sent a message to Marika. All the children were out now with no casualties, but the assault on the compound had just begun. No news of David Joshua yet.' It was brief and to the point, but Marika expected more news would be sent in the morning.

Sherebar knew looking after this many traumatised children was not going to be an easy task, but Marika would cope. Where possible, their parents would be found, but Thor had much larger facilities elsewhere using humans as slave labour. There were rumours that some had already been sent abroad. It had been noticed that Hawk flights had increased over the last few weeks to Africa, which was now mostly controlled by Thor.

Another problem was that this operation would alert Thor to the power Sherebar had, and would certainly make Thor look at their defences. But they had to get David Joshua out before Thor decided to move him. Marika just hoped Val and the others succeeded. She had fond memories of the time they stayed with her before all the carnage of the virus.

CHAPTER THIRTY-NINE

Buster and Cassie had accompanied the children and they would be looked after by Marika until they could be picked up by Val and Jenny. At least with the dogs and children safe they could concentrate on finding David Joshua, thought Josh with a sigh of relief, noticing that what looked like snowflakes, were falling on the building near the control room, which contained the Apis. The snowflake like material got denser and soon had the building covered. So thick nothing could escape.

'That's Joe,' said Josh when Ella queried what was happening. 'He's using a spray from his Black Hawk. He had to stop the Apis escaping, but that has alerted the control room, so all hell could break loose in a minute, if The General and his troops aren't ready.'

Then they heard it. First softly, rising to a crescendo.

What's that? asked Lewis, 'it sounds like singing, how odd.'

'It is singing,' agreed Josh in amazement. 'The noise is causing a vibration. the buildings are shaking, some of the walls have split. Pull your helmets lower to protect your ears, we need to go, this may be our opening.'

Keeping to the shadows they moved stealthily to the centre of the compound.

Val, Edward, Doug, and Jenny were already there.

'Put these identifiers on,' said Jenny handing four buttons to Josh.

'Where should we put them?' asked Josh, handing one each to Ginny, Lewis, and Ella.

'On your left shoulder, they will automatically stick on and will identify you to The General's men,' said Jenny. 'We don't want you getting shot.'

'I know you are getting fidgety Val, but we need to keep to the General's plan,' said Jenny gently, knowing how stressed her sister was about finding her son. 'These four will be best to find him,' indicating Josh and the others. 'We need to get all the captives out before the buildings collapse. The vibrations are working, I admit I was sceptical when I heard about it, but it's working.'

'We have to go now', interrupted Doug urgently, hearing fighting in the distance. 'Good luck you four, we have an hour at the most.'

Dooley Josh's pet rat appeared, ran up Josh's leg to his shoulder and whispered in his ear, 'David Joshua is in the brick building by the hawk hanger, The locks are good and me and my friends haven't been able to get in there.'

Silently they made their way to the building, luckily all guards were now involved in the skirmish with the troops, and Ginny tried to pick the lock. 'I can't do this one,' she said with irritation, 'it's been protected. Can you contact David Joshua, Josh? His mind's blocked to me.'

'His minds blocked to me too. Where's Derebar when you need him?' grumbled Josh. 'He's supposed to keep an eye on David Joshua.'

Derebar was there in the room with David Joshua. Watching the doctor as he got ready to give him another jab. It was something he couldn't let happen, as the boy's small body couldn't take much more of the drug he had been given by his captors. He had managed to fight off the affects so far but was near breaking point. His superior brain, not much help in this situation. He felt Derebar, even in his half-drugged state, and understood what he needed and using his last bit of mind strength he sent a large piece of equipment hurtling towards the doctor knocking him out.

This was just what Derebar needed as he slowly entered the body of the prone doctor. Feeling Josh and Ginny outside he deftly unlocked the door to the amazement of those waiting.

'Quickly,' he said to Josh using the doctor's voice. 'Don't shoot, it's me Derebar. Take David Joshua, can you fly a Hawk? It's the only way out. There are too many of Thor's people to go back the way you came.'

They heard footsteps coming their way, as Josh grabbed David Joshua and the four of them ran to the hanger. Derebar following, used the doctors thumb print to gain access. Just as they reached the Hawk, two of Thor's fighters appeared, firing as they ran towards them. Ginny opened the door as shown by Joe on their training flights and they all piled in closing the door just in time.

'How do we get out of here?' shouted a distressed Lewis as he saw Derebar's doctor shot in the back, and a smoke like mist drift out of the body.

Ginny heard a calm voice in her head saying, 'push the red button, now.' She took one of the two pilot seats and slammed her hand on the red button, the top of the hanger opened, and they were free. Shooting out to the sky.

Josh handed David Joshua over to Lewis and Ella and took the other seat.

'They're following,' said Josh in an even voice. Ginny could feel that he didn't want to show his anxiety to Ella and Lewis. Another Hawk also came shooting out of the hanger adding to their problems.

'Time for a bit of acrobatics,' murmured Ginny, looking at Josh.

He nodded his agreement.

In complete unison they put on a display, twisting and turning with the agility of a bird, which would put some trained pilots to shame. Dodging the guns and rays.

Then unexpectedly help came out of the blue as a large Black Hawk guns blazing, destroying the following Hawk, which fell to earth in a blaze of fire, lighting up the night sky.

'Joe,' whispered Ginny, realising he had saved their lives.

'Follow me,'. 'We need to get urgent help for David Joshua.' said Joe using their usual mind connection. 'Val and the others know we have him,'. 'When I say hover, press the green button and we will guide you in. It's only ten minutes away.'

Arriving at their destination and following Joe's instructions, they entered the underground hanger and opened the door. Steps appeared, and as they disembarked Sally was waiting with an orderly pushing a pod full of light.

'Hey, little man,' she said as she gently took David Joshua from Lewis. 'We will soon have you well again. Josh, Sherebar's in the operation control room, if you all want to see him.'

'Will he be okay?' Ginny asked with tears in her voice, indicating David Joshua as he was put in the pod.

Sally didn't want to give Josh and Ginny false hope, but she said with some conviction. 'He's in the best place for him, and he can self -heal. We just need to wake that part of him up.' She gave them a smile of encouragement and wheeled the pod down the corridor into a room that shone with a green light as the door opened.

The small group looked tired and emotionally drained. Lewis and Ella followed Josh and Ginny as they walked through large rooms that looked like laboratories and others with machines, lights, and walls with changing scenes of galaxies, planets, and unrecognisable lands, pulsing with strange sounds and music.

'It's like something out of an old fantasy film.' Lewis still a bit shaky from his recent experiences, said to Ella in awe. 'I never in my wildest dreams thought I would ever be here doing this. I'm relieved we survived. After all we've been through it's amazing to be here, but I would rather not go through all that trauma again.'

Ella took his hand and gave it a squeeze feeling grateful to be alive and overawed herself.

CHAPTER FORTY

Back in the compound Val and the others watched the display above with trepidation. The falling Hawk lit up the sky and momentarily fighting stopped giving them a chance to run to the underground holding centres. Which had already been logged by The General. Was her baby in that? Val wondered as her stomach churned with the terror of it, when she heard Joe's calm voice,

'He's fine Val. Just being checked over by Sally. Do what you're there for, and I'll update you later.' No point in worrying her now Joe realised. Telling her little boy was in a deep coma wouldn't help anyone in the current situation. He kept that thought well hidden. He didn't want either Jenny or Val reading that bit of his mind.

Edward led them to the building having been informed by Joe's intelligence Informers, was the entrance to the labyrinth. Fighting with Thor was concentrated on the area by the factories and laboratories. With only one or two fighters in their area. The General's strategy had been to try and draw the conflict away from the place the captives were held. Always alert Jenny saw the gunman before he was aware of them, and he was quickly silenced by Jenny's dart.

The door to the building was open as if someone had left in a hurry. Val scanned the area, and when she was sure it was empty Jenny and Doug silently descended the stairs hidden in a corner. These ended in a long corridor lined with sturdy steel doors, bolted from the outside. Val and Edward stood guard at the top of the stairs ready to direct the expected flood of captives.

Doug went quickly along the corridor, unbolting the doors as he went. Jenny followed behind opening them and indicating to the people huddled inside to start moving out, as she tried to make them understand they needed to hurry.

There were so many in each dark, cell like room, the smell was awful. All in the same smock-like top and loose trousers in a dull grey. Some were emancipated, others looked in reasonable condition. Doug knew he would have to check them out when he managed to get out of this hell-hole and somewhere safe.

'We are here to help you,' Jenny said, as loudly as she could. 'You need to go up the stairs quickly. You will be directed to transport that will take you to safety.' She glanced behind her briefly and her hand shook, the stress was getting to her. 'I can't explain anymore just now but you must hurry. Please hurry.' With urgency in her voice, as they had to get out of here now.

As the captives began to realise what was happening, and this may be their only chance of freedom. They started to push towards the doors causing a bottleneck at the top of the stairs. Val and Edward quickly directed them outside to an opening in the fence. Where coaches we're waiting to take them to the safe place holding the children. Jenny and Doug quietly expressed concern at the time it was taking to get the captives out, although it was understandable with the number of people being freed.

'They are sure to be noticed by Thor soon,' hissed Jenny under her breath to Doug. 'The consequences will be devastating if they're caught. Not good for us either'.

'Hurry back,' Val messaged Jenny's mind. 'It's taking too long; you'll have to let those left make their own way out.'

'All out,' Jenny messaged back, 'just coming.'

The last person was on the coach when fighting erupted around them. Doug, Jenny, Edward, and Val ran out dart guns blazing. As the vibrations intensified and buildings started to collapse all around them.

Debris flew through the air making it hard to see and breathe. The coaches sped off, bullets bouncing off the sides, wheels self-inflating as Thor tried to stop them by aiming at the wheels.

'Val's down and Doug's been hit too,' shouted Edward as the Generals fighters surrounded them.

'It's my shoulder. I can still run shouted' Doug. His voice resonating in pain. 'Can you carry Val? She needs help,' he said urgently.

'Yes,' replied Edward as he picked her up in horror. She was bleeding and unconscious, but one look from Doug told him they needed to move now.

'We'll cover you; do you have transport near?' asked one of the fighters.

Then, the van Josh had left for them, silently drew up beside them. They didn't have time to wonder how it managed that. Edward took the driver's seat, after laying Val gently in the back.

Jenny and Doug jumped in, and Doug retrieved the first-aid box stowed in the back. Edward put the vehicle into camouflage mode and the van disappeared to the amazement of the fighters helping them.

'Doug, you need to see to that arm first,' said Jenny, 'It looks as if it has a bullet in it.'

Doug took a syringe from the pack and injected it in his arm.

'That'll help for a while,' said Doug. 'I need to see to Val first.'

He stemmed the blood; 'the bullet missed her heart,' he said, 'but she needs surgery quickly, we need to get her home as fast as possible.'

'I'll give her something to make her comfortable, Warn Dr Foster to make the operating theatre ready. Jenny, contact Sherebar and see if he can help,' he said urgently.

'Will she be okay?' asked Edward the fear showing in his voice.

'Yes,' said Doug reassuringly, but privately he realised he needed to operate as soon as possible, how he was going to do that with his arm in the state it was he wasn't quite sure.

Jenny tried to contact Val's mind but there was silence. 'Val talk to me,' she pleaded tears streaming down her face.

The journey was fraught, and Doug was concerned that he was losing Val. His arm was also causing him a problem. He knew he may have trouble that needed to be sorted soon. *Please let us be in time* he thought as they arrived.

Two of Sherebar's team were waiting, already in operating scrubs, as Val was rushed into the larger of the two small operating theatres. Doug was helped out of the van, by Jenny, and collapsed onto the ground, blood spouting from the wound.

'Doug,' cried Jenny in anguish, as Alistair and Hannah rushed out of the lab.

'Call Dr Foster.' Shouted an agitated Alistair to Edward.

'We'll take Doug to the theatre used for animal operations. It's well equipped. Hannah, stay with Jenny and Doug, I'll get a stretcher from the store.'

By this time some of the villagers had arrived and helped Alister to gently lift Doug onto the stretcher and into the theatre. Dr Foster arrived with two nurses from the village and shooed everyone out of the way while he gowned up and washed his hands.

Hannah and Alistair took Edward and Jenny into the lab's recreation room. Both were in shock. Jenny was so concerned that Val's brain was showing no activity, and that she couldn't read Doug's mind either. She put her head between her knees and gave way to the fear she felt, her body shaking with tension.

Edward paced up and down the small room sweat pouring from his body, fearful that he would lose both Val and his son. He felt so helpless. Time seemed to have stopped, although it had been only an hour since they arrived. Hannah put her arms round Jenny as Alister went to investigate a noise outside. He watched in amazement as a craft seemed to hover above and then slowly descend to the ground, the side slid open. Two orderlies in white coats jumped out pulling a pod like contraption behind them. One of Sherebar's team of doctors came out to meet them and they all went into the operating theatre.

Val was laid in the pod by the doctors and the lid shut. One of the doctors went with her as the pod was loaded into the Hawk while the other indicated to Edward that he should go too.

Then the Doctor left behind turned round and entered the smaller operation theatre.

The villagers, by now quite a large group, watched in awe as the Hawk took to the sky with what seemed exceptional speed and disappeared.

'Do you know what's happened Alistair?' asked one villager as they gathered round him for news.

'I only know what I've been told by Jenny, and she's stressed and upset,' answered Alistair. 'But from what I understand, the country still has a functioning army, and they met Val and the others, at the compound of a group called Thor.' He took a large breath to steady himself, as he was worried about Val. She was a good boss and he admired her. Then he continued, 'there was a fight, and the children and adults held there were freed. They were being held as slave labour. I don't know who controls Thor or what they do. Thor tried to kidnap my Mum, Dad, and Ella, to get at me. Val and the others saved them. Thor are a dangerous group. We are so lucky to live here.'

There was a murmur of agreement from those around him, as if at last, the dissenters were beginning to realise how fortunate they had been. 'In the fight against Thor, Val, and Doug were injured Jenny told me, but Thor's compound was destroyed,' said Alistair with a sigh.

'Why did they put themselves in danger if we have an army?' asked another villager.'

'Thor had kidnapped David Joshua,' replied Alistair. 'But Ginny and Josh found him. He's at the same place they're taking Val, but I don't know how he is, no one will say. We must help keep the village functioning, so that Val and David Joshua, have somewhere to come back to. I'm not sure how Ginny and Josh are, but I know with Ella and Lewis they rescued the children and David Joshua.'

'I'd like to know how Ginny and Josh did that, sometime.

Those two seem to have something special, for youngsters,' said a man in the group.

'Your sister and Lewis aren't far behind them, are they?' enquired a villager.

'I'm happy Ella found some good friends. They are special, but just youngsters. The reality could have been so different if for Ella if she hadn't come here.' replied Alister, as he got ready to go back to work, and the villagers dispersed.

CHAPTER FORTY-ONE

The Hawk taking Val entered the hanger and Val was rushed in her pod to the same room as David Joshua. There were medical staff waiting for her, and she was quickly surrounded by a golden light.

'Her life source is low,' commented one orderly. 'But being with her son may help, his body is beginning to cope with the drugs he was given, if he can wake his healing ability, he may be able to help his mum. He's so young it's not fully developed,' he added on a sombre note.

Edward was now sitting in a small room outside, trying to control his emotions. His mind went back to when he first met Val, He'd always liked her, she had been the farms vet, and was forever trying to persuade him and his dad to use her more natural methods and open an organic farm shop and cafe. It took him a long while to pluck up the courage to ask her out, as he was sure he didn't have a chance with her. He thought she was so beautiful and vibrant and out of his league. She asked him to a meal with others, including Dr Foster, beating him to it, and it went from there. When he had the accident, (which he was sure Derebar caused,) that allowed Derebar to invade his body. The little piece of him still conscious, had to watch his life taken over. That was the worst time of his life until now.

It was only when they all met at a remote holiday centre for safety, having already had skirmishes with Thor, that Sherebar realised what was happening, and managed to free him from Derebar's spirit. It had been a stressful time, as he had also learnt Val was pregnant with David Joshua.

During the time Derebar had control of his body, Edward had to reluctantly admit to himself, that Derebar, using his special powers, had done a lot to make the village secure for what was to come. He realised that had been done for David Joshua's sake, and not any wish on Derebar's side, to help the villagers.

Edward knew all the dramas that he and Val had been through made their love stronger. He loved Val and his son with a passion he hadn't known he was capable of and was not sure if he would be able to continue without them. He didn't know if he believed in a God, but he silently prayed anyway. Tears slid down his face unchecked. Nothing mattered to him more than Val and his son in the next room.

Then suddenly he heard his voice in his head. 'Daddy don't worry, I'll look after Mummy.'

Edward rushed out of the room just as Ginny and Josh walked down the corridor.

'He spoke to me, David Joshua spoke to me, I must tell the doctors.' said an agitated Edward, his voice breaking with emotion. 'Where are the doctors?'

Just then a doctor came out of a room and beckoned Edward, as Edward reached him, he put an arm round Edwards's shoulder, and led him into the room where the pods holding David Joshua and Val were. The doctor gently opened the boy's pod, and David Joshua slowly opened his arms. As Edward picked him up, he buried his head in his dad's shoulder his arms tightly wound round Edwards's neck. Edward held the boy's small body close to his, relishing his warmth. Murmuring over and over how he now understood the grief of those who'd lost a child and was thankful that his child had survived.

The doctor said gently. 'David Joshua must rest, but you can stay with him now. You both need to talk to Val.' Indicating the chair by the pod Val was lying in. 'Tell her your feelings, tell her how much you love her and that you can't manage without her, she must decide what to do, and if she wants to stay here. She needs to feel your love.'

Val was floating on what looked like white clouds it was soft and comfortable, and she felt safe and happy. She didn't feel scared, but somehow connected to others in the same situation. She sensed someone was trying contact her, but she didn't want to listen, it became more insistent, then she felt waves of love that were becoming difficult to ignore. She had vague memories of a child and a man she was connected to. They were calling her back, but did she want to go? She had a decision to make, then suddenly she knew what she wanted to do.

Val opened her eyes and looked at Edward and said, 'It was so peaceful Edward. The problems of the world seemed so small. It was as if I understood everything and I wanted to stay, but then I felt the pull of you and our boy and I knew I couldn't leave you. I want to go back to my animals and natural remedies and leave Alistair to run the laboratories, and I am expecting our baby,' she said suddenly. 'She's going to be called Star.'

'A child?' queried Edward in amazement, trying to take it all in. 'I thought Sherebar said no babies were being born.'

'Well one is,' said Val with a smile. 'I'm happy to be back, but I don't want to fight any more. Let's leave it to the Josh's and Ginny's of the world.' She stopped in thought for a minute and sighed. 'Although until Thor's defeated there won'tt be any peace so we may not have any choice,' before promptly falling asleep.

Edward was stunned. He looked at David Joshua in his arms and for the first time felt that it could be possible, to make a place in the world his children could live in. If Thor could be defeated would that be a reality? That was something he didn't know the answer to, but he felt hopeful with the help of those around him, they could make a difference.

'What was that all about?' commented Ginny. As she watched Edward enter David Joshua's recovery room.

'I think he's awake,' answered Josh in a whisper.

'Has he contacted you?' queried Ginny. 'I've tried but had no luck.'

'I caught a murmur but no more,' replied Josh.

'Let's find Sherebar and find out what's happening. We've lost Ella and Lewis somewhere in the maze of rooms too,' said Ginny with a grimace. 'I wonder what they think of all the stuff here. It's a bit unbelievable when you see all the installations and screens for the first time.'

They found Sherebar in the control room talking to Ella and Lewis.

'I was just coming to find you,' he said smiling, as an aggravated Ginny whispered to Josh, 'He could have just sent us a message and told us Ella and Lewis where we were.' Forgetting for a moment Sherebar could, when he wished to, read her mind too.

'Marika's just going to give us an update and I thought you may like to hear what she got to say,' said Sherebar, smiling to himself, and clearly aware of Ginny's irritation.

'What about David Joshua?' asked Josh with tension in his voice. 'Edwards with him now but we don't know how he's doing.'

'His brain is waking up and he is sending strength to his Mum, he will be fine,' asserted Sherebar, 'but Val needs his help. After we have heard what Marika has to say we will go and add our energy to his.'

'We should do that now,' said Ginny angrily, 'we can talk to Marika later.'

'Just now all Val needs is David and Edward,' said Sherebar soothingly. 'They will give her a strong urge to live., We have to wait. We don't want to confuse that energy.'

'Okay,' said Ginny slumping in a chair, she wanted to do something now, but she understood in her heart Sherebar would do everything to save Val. It wasn't easy for her; she didn't like inaction. Val, Edward, Hannah, and the others had become her family and she was beginning to realise how much they all meant to her. They had taken Tip, Bel, and her to their hearts and treated them like Josh. She didn't love easily but knew she would always love them too.

Josh put a comforting arm around her shoulders. 'I love Val too,' he said, 'but I can feel David Joshua wakening. can't you? He's going to need us when he comes home. It won't be easy for him.'

Ginny nodded 'I didn't want to believe he was awake and then find it was wrong, so haven't said anything.'

CHAPTER FORTY-TWO

Little did everyone know that Buster and Cassie had been doing their own thing at the place where the children were staying. They were finding it exhausting being with so many children, much as they loved them, and were just looking for somewhere to escape to when they a found a young girl hiding behind the curtains sobbing quietly to herself.

Buster and Cassie went up close to her, Buster putting a paw on her lap and Cassie licking away her tears.

The young girl put her arms round Cassie as she continued to shake with emotion.

'I want my Mummy. Will I ever see my Mummy again?' she cried.

Buster looked at Cassie, pointed his nose in the air and sniffed.

'Look after her Cass, I've just had an idea,' said Buster, communicating with Cassie in the usual way, as he pushed open the door and silently went down the empty corridor, up some stairs and into a room full of adults. They didn't take much notice of him, most still shocked from their ordeal.

He wandered round the room, is nose in the air until he found the person with the odour he wanted. She was sitting down, vacant eyed and so white she looked hardly alive her cheeks wet with tears.

Buster pulled on her joggers trying to get her to understand he wanted her to go with him, but she ignored him.

'He wants you to go with him,' said a man sitting nearby. 'I'll go with you if it makes you feel better. It doesn't look as if he will go away until you do.'

She shook her head and listlessly but got up and followed Buster out of the room. He led her slowly down the stairs and as they began walking along the corridor, Cassie came out of a door with Beth.

Buster and Cassie both stopped as the eyes of the girl and woman met.

'Beth is it you?' cried the woman softly holding out her arms, her voice full of emotion. 'I didn't think I'd see you again.'

'Mummy', sobbed Beth as she ran into her arms.

Just then, Marika stepped into the hall taking in the scene and noting the two dogs. Buster laid down, his head between his paws, Cassie by his side.

An exasperated Marika looked at them both. 'What am I going to do with you both? We needed to do this in a controlled way, I'll talk to you later.' With that she walked up to Beth and her mother and gently led them away.

'What do we do now?' said Buster, 'we only wanted to help.'

Cassie went up to him and licked his ear. Urging him to follow her back to the children. Slowly, his ears and tail down, Buster followed her back to the noisy children's room. He wanted to go home.

CHAPTER FORTY-THREE

Lewis and Ella were quiet, this was such a new experience for them. They had seen amazing machines and how the unused part of the human brain could be used. It was science fiction come to life. It was exciting and a bit scary, but Lewis especially had told Ella that this new life was much more interesting and exciting than his old one. This place was a revelation and not something he would ever forget.

Ella had an inkling of what her mind could do but wasn't as advanced as Josh and Ginny. She understood that Lewis didn't have that kind of mind although he was an amazing engineer. As she was wondering what the future held for them, Marika appeared on the screen in Sherebar's control room.

Dressed in her trademark colourful flowing gowns, her long hair shining and a huge smile. She opened her arms with a welcoming gesture and said, 'I have some good news amid all the sorrow.'

'The children have had breakfast. They seemed to really

appreciate the food and we now have names for them all. Which will help in identifying any family connections,' she smiled as she continued. 'Most of the children were taken from around the county they were kept in, and have been traumatised, but are responding well to the new situation. They are quiet and scared but are beginning to find their voices. I have arranged for small groups at a time to see doctors, but we want to give them space to play and have confidence in us. It's hard for them to trust anyone, so it will take time.' Picking up a tablet with names on, she said. 'We are keeping them apart from the adults rescued, just now, and are also gathering the names of the adults. 'Although we have been able to match some of the children with their parents, as the adults were taken from the same area, there have been no meetings now, except for one. Thanks to two helpful dogs not doing as they were asked. They don't understand this needs to be carefully handled.'

'It will affect the children whose parents are still missing. We must think about housing, food, and work for the adults. Not an easy situation, as there will not be much trust in those trying to rebuild the country.'

'We have learnt that there are still children out there fending for themselves. They are more streetwise, and will be wary of any offers of help because they are aware of children just disappearing.'

With that, she showed the large room where the children were in small groups reading talking, building Lego, or playing games. The rooms were bright and colourful, there were tables with various activities, a table with drinks, biscuits and cakes and several groups listening to stories being told.

'Look', said Ginny. 'That's Buster and Cassie wandering around, we forgot about them in all the commotion. Are they okay Marika?'

'Yes.' said Marika, 'As you know they have minds of their own and decided one young girl needed extra help. I'll update you on this another time, you and can always find Buster if there's food around, but I think they're missing everyone. I'll try and plan for them to be taken home. I'll have more information in a few days when I have more news.'

'Buster and Cassie will be planning to make their own way home if somethings not done about it soon,' said Josh. 'They like to be in the middle of the action and with everything that's happening, Cassie will be aware of David Joshua and Val's situation,'

'Could we come and pick them up on our way back?' asked Josh. 'They look a bit down, which is unusual for them.'

'No problem,' said Sherebar. 'I'm sure we can arrange that. Val will be okay now she's woken up, but it will take time. David Joshua and Edward are helping. Doug and Jenny could probably do with your help in keeping the village safe for now. We will have to wait and see if there's any reaction from Thor to the destruction of their compound. It will take a time for them to reorganise themselves, but we may have to make plans before they've strengthen their defence at their headquarters.'

'See you when we pick up the dogs Marika,' said Josh. Marika smiled and waved as she disappeared from the screen.

Edward had laid David Joshua back in his pod to sleep and went to find the others. He entered the room with a stunned expression on his face. 'What's the matter,' said Ginny anxiously. 'Are they both all right?'

'They're fine and both asleep, but Val has just said she's pregnant, I'm in shock, and David Joshua and Val said the baby's name is Star. How he knows that I don't know. I thought pregnancy wasn't possible just now,' said Edward looking quizzically at Sherebar.

'Well, it looks as if I was wrong,' said Sherebar with a little smile. 'I'm not infallible, but I do still think it won't be so easy to have children now. We will have to wait and see, but this is promising news. We know that even those immune and vaccinated have been exposed to the virus, and that men might now only be able to sire a small number of children. There can't be a population explosion again if the earth wants to survive.'

~

Everyone was silent for a moment before Ginny burst out. 'If we have to leave, can we take a Hawk?' she asked cheekily. Knowing the answer would probably be no.

Sherebar looked at her and laughed. 'What do you think Ginny? Do you expect Joe to let you take one of his precious Hawks?'

'But we bought you an extra one, can't we take that?' she answered.

'We need them all here if we are going to tackle Thor,' said Sherebar seriously. 'The General will be here soon, and we need to discuss what happens next,'

'We want to help,' interrupted Josh. 'We can't stop now,'

'I know,' replied Sherebar with a sigh, understanding they would want to be involved in whatever was decided to do next. 'If we go for Thor's headquarters it will be a challenge, but the times not right yet. I promise I will involve you in what's happening, but for now you need to pick up the dogs and go home. Four of The General's men who are here, will go with you in case of trouble and to bring the vehicle back, you will need two vans. These will be ready tomorrow. Marika will expect you all.'

CHAPTER FORTY-FOUR

The next day after saying goodbye to Sherebar and Edward two vans were ready to go. There were three of the Generals men in one, and the other one in the van with Josh, Ginny, Ella, and Lewis.

'Well, that was an interesting visit,' said Lewis as he got into the van. 'I'd like to learn more; it could be useful. It's a bit overwhelming and a lot to take in, but it would be helpful to find out more about the new technology they have here.'

'So would I,' agreed Ella. 'Perhaps the four of us could talk about it when we get home,' realising as she said it, that the village and the people there were where her home was now. She didn't miss her old life at all, that meant she was growing up at last. Alistair would be pleased as he was settled in the village and wanted them all to stay there, join him, and make a new home.

'Wow look at this,' indicated Ginny as she took her seat in the front of the van. There were two sets of controls and numerous dials indicating the programmed route and all the security features. 'I'd like time to explore these more.' she said. 'It almost makes up for not using the Hawk.' There were also two side windows blacked out, but still making the outside visible to those seated behind the drivers.

Josh got in the other front seat. 'Ready to go?' he asked. 'It says here,' pointing to the lighted display panel, 'two hours ten minutes so this must go fast. Seat belts on? Marika here we come.' With that he pushed start, and the van slowly drew away.

They were about an hour into their journey when Ginny suddenly put her hands over her ears. 'We must stop, can't you feel it, Josh?'

'What's happening?' asked the officer in the van with them, 'why are we slowing down.'

'Someone's in trouble,' said Ginny. 'There's a lot of fear and stress about. Can you see anything Josh?'

The van came to a halt and the men in the van behind got out to find out what was happening.

Josh sat with his eyes closed and Ginny put her hand to her lips to warn the others to be quiet.

He gradually opened his eyes. 'I've sent a message to Joe, and he said ask the van what's around, press the blue button. You're better at visualising Ginny, focus on what you're feeling that may give us an idea of what to do.'

The van system brought up a map showing a building three hundred metres away, it was pulsing red.

'It looks like a medical facility,' said Ginny, 'I see ambulances and women in beds. That's where the distress and fear is coming from.'

'We need to look,' said the officer indicating the other three soldiers. 'You four stay here,' Looking straight at Ginny.

'No way,' said Josh, 'we're all in this together.'

The Officer looked at the other men and one gave a slight nod.

Ginny said suddenly. 'There's only one security guard. The rest are orderlies and doctors of some kind. They think they are safe from discovery here.'

'We need to get closer.' said the Officer. 'The maps are indicating that there's a band of trees to the right of the building. Can you get our vans there without being seen?' he asked Josh and the other driver.

'If your van's the same as ours, we can,' said Josh. This van has the same camouflage option as the other one I drove. It's quiet too.'

'Let's go then,' said the Officer.

They managed to get to the trees without detection and spread out around the building. Keeping out of range of the cameras that had been noted. It had only two entrances, and was a two-story brick building with space in the roof. Windows on the sides and cameras on the back and front. Two skylights on the roof were open. and what looked like hot air, coming out in a plume of smoke, of a vent in the roof.

'How do we get in without raising the alarm? asked Josh. If we disable the cameras someone we don't want to meet, will be here soon.'

'I can get onto the roof,' said the Officer.

'So can I,' agreed Ginny, looking at several pipes running vertically to the roof. 'Those pipes will make it easy. We could open the windows to let you in if we can get there undetected.'

The Officer agreed. 'We'll try that first. If we get caught, go in the front. I just want to sort this with as little trauma as possible. Just make sure no one can raise the alarm.'

Ginny was up the pipe in a flash, followed by the Officer. They waved to others below and entered the building by the skylight. Dropping silently to the floor and looking around,

Ginny waited for the Officer. The room was long, with wires everywhere. The floor was layered with dust and didn't look as if it was in constant use. Odd tables and equipment pilled to one side.

'Look,' said the Officer pointing to a box on the wall. 'The control box for the electrics. A bit of an out of the way place to put it, but it can help us if I can rig the alarm so it doesn't send out distress signals. It looks quite old fashioned. They must feel under the radar here to have left it without updating.'

'Can you, do it?' asked Ginny, 'we don't have much time. The distress I'm feeling is getting worse.'

Taking two tools out of the utility belt all the soldiers had on, the Officer went to the box, and within two minutes had redirected the cameras and opened all the electric windows.

'Quick,' he said, 'let Josh know the windows are open and we will join them as soon as possible.'

Ginny sent the message, then followed the Officer out of the door.

They silently went down the stairs without a problem. Just as they were going to turn round a corner, they heard someone coming. The footsteps stopped and as the Officer peered round it, he saw the back of someone entering a room.

Ginny whispered to him. 'They're talking about moving some patients out, we may have arrived here just in time. Josh and the others are coming. No problems so far.'

Josh asked Ginny. 'Can you get to the ground floor? We've disabled the security guard. The main wards are here, and this is where most of the distress is coming from.'

'We need to deal with the staff here first, there are several in a room having a meeting, then we'll be down,' replied Ginny, as the Officer took a small canister from his belt.

'It's an effective form of anaesthetic,' he said to Ginny's

querying look. 'It'll put them to sleep for a while, but we need to make sure we don't breath the spray in. I'm hoping the doctors will be so engrossed in the meeting they won't notice it until too late. It's fast acting.'

They crept along the corridor to the room Ginny indicated, the Officer activated the canister, gingerly opened the door, and placed the canister on the floor.

'What's that? I thought I heard a noise,' said one of the group of doctors.

'I don't feel right,' said another as he slipped off his chair. One by one the anaesthetic effected them all.

Ginny and the Officer quickly checked that they were all down and asleep, then made their way to join the others.

'This is where most of the distress is coming from.' said Josh as he carefully opened the doors to what looked like the entrance to the hospital wards. He then opened the other door and went into the ward, nodding to the Officer, stopping for a moment to take in the full horror before him. They stood transfixed for a moment, not believing what they were seeing.

Rows of beds with women who were hooked up to machines that looked as if they were taking blood. It was like something out of an old horror movie.

'Get out,' shouted a doctor. 'What are you doing here?' He pressed a button on the wall. Looking surprised when the alarm didn't ring.

'That won't work,' said the officer with a grim smile. 'We've disabled all your alarms. My men will round up any other Doctors or orderlies we find. Some have already been taken out of action. I advise you to co-operate, that way you won't be hurt.' To the others he said. 'I've warned Joe, and he will be here in a Black Hawk soon. He's bringing our own doctors and will take the weakest women back with him.' Taking a deep breath as even, with so much experience he had been shaken with the view of the wards. He continued, 'those remaining should be taken in the ambulances outside to Marika. We have disabled the drivers and other personnel; they won't be waking up for a few hours yet. Get to it,' he said briskly to his men. 'We don't have much time.'

Ginny walked over to the captives for it was clear they weren't willing patients and tried to send messages of calm to them. Touching them gently and whispering they were going somewhere safe. Eyes followed her as she went down the beds.

The Doctor made a dash for the door but found his way blocked by one of the soldiers.

Ginny no longer able to contain herself, sent a spike of pain to his head. Causing him to double over in agony. 'See how you like it; I thought your motto was Do No Harm,' she said ignoring Josh's warning glance.

'Joes arrived,' Josh said, feeling the familiar energy of an arriving Hawk. 'What are we going to do with these doctors?' Pointing to those incapacitated.

'Leave them here, perhaps put them on their own machines, see how they like it,' said the Officer. 'We need to deal with the women first.'

Joe and four of Sherebar's doctors came into the ward, taking in the sight, acknowledged those there, and got to work without a word.

It took some time to unhook the women safety, some comatose and others unable to talk. Most didn't understand what was happening despite Ginny's calming words. Loading the women needing immediate attention into the Hawks medicine bay, was efficient and quickly complete.

'We need to get these back for assessment as soon as possible,' said Joe indicating the captive women, and giving Josh and Ginny a hug. 'Well done to find them I don't think they would have lasted another session of this treatment; the others can be taken in the ambulances outside. Don't forget to disable the trackers on them first though. Will talk to you when you're at Marika's.' With that he left.

Loading the remaining victims in the ambulances and vans took some time. Ella and Lewis's had already disabled the trackers on the ambulances, as they had stayed with the vans to keep them safe if there was trouble.

Each of the soldiers took an ambulance, leaving as they were filled up, The Officer driving the other van, leaving Josh, Ginny, Lewis, and Ella to continue in the one they had been driving.

Against Ginny's inclination, all the staff had been left disabled in the facility without communication, doors locked, and the machines smashed.

'Let's go,' said Josh as he got in the van after making sure the four stretchers in the back were loaded correctly. The women had been given sedatives to make sure their journey was as comfortable as possible.

'Lewis was it difficult to disable the trackers?' asked Josh. 'Dooley usually does that for us, but she'd decided to find her own way home after the last incident with Thor. I'm not sure if she went with Jenny. I'll ask Mum if she got home okay. In all the action and emotion, I forgot to ask, and feel bad about that now, she's been through a lot with me.'

Lewis had been amazed at how the animals in the family seemed to understand and work with everyone. He said with a grin. 'I disabled all trackers, and the outside security wires too. Anyone coming here may get a bit of a shock literally, when they eventually release those in the building,'

It took longer than Josh hoped to get to Marika's building, as they were conscious of their patients in the back. Once there they were greeted by two thankful dogs who jumped in the van as soon as the front doors were opened and refused to move.

Marika had been ready and sent out some of her staff to gently transfer the women to a comfortable room with several beds. Doctors were in attendance to help them settle, although the women shrunk in fear as the doctors approached. Marika walked among them spreading calm as she went.

'Marika we'll take the dogs out of your way and be off. It seems a long time since we've been home, and Toby will be missing Cassie and Buster. I hope they haven't been too much trouble,' said Josh with a grin as they walked out, knowing Cassie and Buster had their own way of helping.

Marika raised her eyebrows, but Buster and Cassie did have a special place in her heart, and they knew she couldn't be cross with them for long. She waved as they all left and went back to her patients.

CHAPTER FORTY-FIVE

Buster kept licking Ginny's ear as they drove back, but Cassie was subdued.

'Val's going to be fine Cassie,' said Ginny gently seeing her ears down and her tail curled under her, understanding from her body language she was worried about Val. 'She'll be home soon, so will David Joshua, Buster stop that, you're making my hair wet.'

'I'm just happy to be going home,' said Buster to himself. Letting out a big sigh as he stopped licking Ginny. 'I hope they have some proper food for us too, dogs were not meant to be vegetarian.'

They were all unusually quiet on the drive back all lost in their own thoughts and were thankful when they eventually reached the village. Ginny let Lewis, Ella, and the dogs out, Josh parked the van and both he and Ginny gave a sigh of relief to be home. Hannah rushed out giving them both a hug and said, 'I've food ready for anyone who wants it, and I'll update you on Val. Come on lets go home.'

Buster nudged Cassie. 'I hope that means us too. Cassie cheer up, you can feel David Joshua and Val are okay,

Hannah's bound to have food for us too, and we can see Toby.' said Buster nudging her to follow him.

Val was home but Doug was insisting that she stayed in bed for a few more days. David Joshua was with Edward, as he found it difficult to let him out of his sight. He couldn't put the horror of the fact he nearly lost them both out of his mind. David Joshua, thankful that Edward couldn't read his mind, wanted to be with Josh and Ginny, but understood his Dad needed him now.

~

Val was sitting up in bed talking to Jenny. 'I hope Sherebar, and The General can deal with the other Thor compound,' she said worriedly to Jenny. 'I don't think I can go through that again.'

'Nor can I,' agreed Jenny. 'Do you think we'll ever get back to something like normal?'

'I'm not sure, but I'm going back to my practice,' said Val. 'We must be able to find other survivors on farms or small holdings. Joe said most farm animals were surviving so someone will be looking after them. The towns were worst hit by the virus, according to Sally. Farms will become more important as food supplies dwindle. Luckily there are still ways to transport food. There won't be such a variety of choice available, but it needs organising. Perhaps that's something the Generals men can do.'

'Alistair is going to run the labs, so I won't have to do that,' said Val exhaustion in her voice. What about you and Doug? Have you thought about what you want to do?'

'We like it here,' answered Jenny,' but Doug wants to look at the nearest hospital to us, to see what kind of shape it's in. Some of his old partners have been in touch and want to start again, but out of London. They were all safe as vaccinated, and there are other medical staff who can manage the hospitals there. London's devastated with so many empty buildings and with a reduced population to look after there, they want to meet to discuss a possible future here.'

'The Government are gradually organising the cities, but no one here is going to blindly follow any directives given any more, are they?'

'No,' said Val with a laugh. 'Can you imagine Ginny and Josh and the others obeying any rules they don't believe in.'

'Good luck to the Government if they try,' agreed Jenny with a smile.

'They are using the empty tower blocks as sort of greenhouses though, so Joe said and they're quite successful.' mused Val. 'The entrepreneur spirit is still alive and well. He sent pictures and some tower blocks have walls of green showing, including flowers.'

'That's quite inventive, I wonder how they do that'. Said Jenny.

I'm sure Sally would know if you're interested,' answered Val. There was a knock on the door and Hannah entered with a tray of goodies and some homemade sparkling elderflower drink.

'Thought we could have a bit of a girly chat and some spoiling,' she said putting down the tray. 'I bought Cassie back. She wanted to come home.'

CHAPTER FORTY-SIX

Life had been carrying on as usual at the farm and fishing port. Luckily the carnage at the Thor holding compound where Andy had been held, hadn't affected them, and Wilf had promised to take Andy and Timmy fishing.

The sun was shining, the sky blue and if it wasn't for the fact of empty houses and quiet roads, Wilf could almost deceive himself that everything was back to normal. Maggie had packed them lunch and the boys were excited to be doing something different. They walked to the port, it was calm, and several boats were bobbing up and down as the sun sent sunbeams dancing on the sea.

The port was still beautiful, self-seeded flowers blooming in the gardens surrounding it, and the pots around the causeway full of Geraniums, lavender, and Poppies. Jumping on the boat the boys helped Wilf ready the boat to depart. Once out at sea they let out the nets, laughing at the hungry seagulls following hoping for a meal.

Wilf realised how lucky he was to have Maggie and the children, enough food, and a way of providing for them. If it weren't for the fact of not knowing what had happened to his son and grandchild, he would be happy. That was a tremendous change to how both he and Maggie had felt before Andy and his friends arrived.

'Do you want to eat now?' he asked the boys, who nodded their heads in unison making Wilf smile. 'Let's see what we have'. There were thick crusty sandwiches with cheese and butter from Timmy's farm, cooked prawns, and lettuce and tomatoes from the garden. There was even cake made with flour from Val's village and eggs from the chickens that roamed around the garden. Wilf marvelled at how when necessity called, the children changed their diet and didn't seem to hunker after McDonald's or Kentucky fried chicken anymore.

'I think we've caught something,' shouted Andy with excitement in his voice as he watched the net moving. They helped Wilf haul in the net and poured the contents in the waiting tanks, there were crabs and fish the boys couldn't identify but Wilf assured them it was all delicious to eat. 'Fish and chips tonight boys,' Wilf said with satisfaction. The boys danced around the boat singing at the top of their voices. Hearing them, a seed of an idea began to form in Wilf's mind. They took their time sailing back watching the seals dancing in the water as if they were joining in the boy's song. When they arrived at the port it took a while to load the fish into the wheelie containers waiting, and to put the fish in the fridges in one of Wilf's outhouses. Luckily Wilf a practical person, had the foresight to instal independent sola power, and electric wind generators. The electric grid was still working in some places but was intermittent.

As they arrived Maggie looked at Wilf and silently motioned to him to leave the boys and come into the front room they seldom used. In the room was an older man and a young man. Both casually dressed. 'They say they are Andy's brother and father,' said Maggie as the older man held out his hand to Wilf.

'How do I know you're who you say you are?' asked Wilf. 'I don't want Andy, or the other children upset.'

'My wife and I were kidnapped and taken to a compound where we were separated. The conditions were terrible, and I worked in one of the kidnappers' factories. It was hard work and not much food. I was distraught when my wife and I were separated and worried about what would happen to Andy and Jason. Then one day after we were locked in by our captors for the evening, someone unlocked the doors and shouted at us to get out and run quickly to some coaches. We weren't sure what to do, but anywhere was better than staying, so we went. There was fighting outside, and it was terrifying. The coaches drove to a large building, where the rooms and staff were welcoming. We were given food and shown where we could shower and find clean clothes. It was as if we were human beings again. The next day they took our names and information about families, and later told me there was a young man calling himself Jason who had the same name.'

Jason interrupted, 'I was shaking, and so traumatised that I couldn't believe at first that Dad was there. When we met, we couldn't stop hugging each other but it was tearing us apart not having news of Mum and Andy. '

Maggie looked at them with concern in her eyes and said. 'The boys are playing games on the old consoles now so won't surface for a while. Why don't you both sit down, and I will get a drink and some food,' as this was always Maggie's way of coping with an emergency. She was worried about these two, they were so thin, and the young man still had this body shake when he got emotional.

After she had plied them with drinks and sandwiches, she asked, 'How did you find Andy?'

'Marika, the woman at the building, knew Andy's story and his name as he was in contact with a man called Sherebar, and this Sherebar recognised our stories matched. She told us where to find you,' said the man.

'What's your name?' asked Wilf.

'Adam,' answered the man. 'I don't want to take Andy away, just to know he's safe is enough. We don't want to go back to our old home but need to find somewhere to live.'

Wilf and Maggie looked at each other and Maggie gave a brief nod.

'How about living here? There are several houses to choose from. The owners won't be back, having found somewhere else they preferred. You could have the pick of them, and we could do with some help here. I know you can sail as Andy told me you taught him, and there is an unused fishing boat in the harbour.'

Just as Adam was going to answer, the door was flung open, and Andy and Timmy came to an abrupt halt in the doorway. Andy not quite believing what he was seeing.

He stopped suddenly and gasped. 'We knew something was going on, didn't we Timmy?' said Andy, there was so much noise in the air. Dad! Jason! How are you here? I didn't think I would see you again,' as he ran tears streaming down his face to his dads' open arms.

A bemused looking Timmy watched the drama unfolding in awe.

'Where's Mum?' asked Andy, shuddering with stress.

. . .

This was the question Adam had been dreading. Holding Andy tighter Adam said, his voice trembling. 'I don't know, the people at the house we were in, said they would try and find her, as more captives were arriving, but that there was still one more facility with captives to find. They were keeping account of names of all adults and children as they arrive and matching them up when they could, but it takes time.'

'Can't we look for her?' Andy asked his eyes full of tears.

'Where would we look? We must leave it to the experts,' answered his dad gently, not letting go of his son.

'Wilf has suggested we look at a house here to possibly stay, would you like that?'

'Yes,' said Andy vehemently his body still shaking. 'This is home now I couldn't leave Maggie and Wilf. My friends are here and It's safe.' He pulled Timmy into the room. 'This is Timmy, his family have a farm near, and there is a village where Val, Josh and Ginny live. They are the ones who helped us.'

'And us too', said Adam, as he noticed Maggie had a tear in her eye when Andy said he couldn't leave them.

'Let's have something to eat with everyone first,' said Maggie as her stomach fluttered and her pulse raced with emotion, clearly not wanting to sway any decisions to be made due to her held back tears. 'I'll call the others and our neighbours, and you can talk to them, to help you make up your mind.'

In the end it was quite a party. Wilf brought out his homemade beer and wine. Others bought an apple pie and Maggie made fish and chips.

After the meal Jason said, 'I don't want to go back to our old house Dad. I want to stay here. Wilf's got a studio and he's going to show it to me later.' So it was decided that he, and his dad, would at least stay for a few days.

'I'm not going anywhere but here,' said Andy mutinously. 'So please look at those houses Dad. I'm not moving.'

Gently releasing Andy, his dad said, 'we'll look, don't worry.' Adam marvelled at the change in the biddable boy he'd known. But was beginning to realise Andy had to fend for himself and was proud of the way Andy had looked after his friends.

CHAPTER FORTY-SEVEN

'Let's go then,' said Wilf taking the keys of the two cottages he wanted to show Adam. But if he expected a quiet tour of them, he hadn't considered that everyone was interested in their possible new neighbour, and wanted to see if he was staying. They didn't want to lose Andy either. The children were part of their new life and future. The first cottage had three bedrooms and a small garden, but the second one had three bedrooms and a small annex, which was perfect for Jason. It also had a large overgrown garden. It was obvious there had also once been a substantial vegetable patch and orchard. A bonus these days.

'What about the people who lived here?' asked Adam.

'They left and won't be coming back,' answered Wilf sorrowfully. 'We're keeping the other cottages safe for the other fishermen that left in case they come back.'

'We'd like to take this one if it's free' said Adam indicating the second cottage they saw. 'What do we do now?'

'Andy, you, and Timmy take your Dad and Jason to the harbour and show your Dad the boats, we'll have a talk here, and let you know what's decided when you get back, Is that okay?'

'Yep,' agreed Andy, 'Come on Dad let's go.' The other children clearly wanted to go too. Andy had confided in Wilf, that he was worried they would be sad that some of their own family hadn't been found, and be different with him, but they acted just the same as usual. They ran around the harbour chasing the chickens that ran around everywhere. Yelling when they found an egg.

Adam asked his Dad, 'what do you think?' as they looked at the fishing boat. 'It's bigger than the yacht we sailed, but a lot of it looks automated and Wilf manages his on his own.'

'I'll help if you need me, especially if it means we can stay here. I'm nervous of us being alone somewhere else,' said Jason with a tremor in his voice. Clearly still not quite believing his good luck at being here.

'We'll tell Wilf, we'll stay then, shall we? if they'll have us. Let's go back and see what has been agreed,' said Adam. 'Andy,' he called, 'we've seen enough, time to go back.'

Andy rounded up the children making sure they didn't drop any eggs as they went. They all piled into the kitchen as Maggie said, 'what great timing, you can all help me dry the dishes and clear up.' She smiled as there was one big groan before they all helped put everything away. 'That wasn't too hard now, was it?' said Maggie before shooing them all into the room holding the adults.

'Dad's smiling so it must be good news,'. Andy murmured to his friends. 'Come on Timmy let's go to my room and see if we can talk to Sherebar or Joe. This is going to get boring, and I want to ask if I should tell Dad and Jason about all the things we are learning to do,' said Andy.

Adam and Jason were welcomed to the fishing community, but it was taking Andy a while to decide where he wanted to live. That's why Wilf though he would get them all involved with a project he'd been thinking of for a few weeks. He got everyone together one evening a bit later and said. 'I don't know if you all know, but Maggie and I used to be in the music industry until it all went pear shaped. We were cancelled on social media for a remark taken out of context. The boys were singing the other day and I realised I missed the music and wondered if we could get the others around here to join in a small concert perhaps on Timmy's farm field, or in the village nearby. '

'I would have to get the boys to check with the people responsible for the village security, to see if it would be safe. I'm not sure if the group holding you have been defeated, but what do you say? We'd have to find musicians and singers but there was a shop in one of the small, abandoned towns that had instruments. If we could salvage them, we may be able to form a band.'

'I was in a band,' said Jason,' don't know how good I'd be now, but I'll audition if you like.'

'First, we must see what instruments are left. Does anyone feel like coming with me to find out?' Said Wilf

'We'll come,' said Andy and Timmy jumping up and down. But Wilf noticed that Adam and Jason were reticent, and realised they were scared to leave the safety of their new home. Past events had understandably made them cautious. 'How about you and the others make space in my studio,' said Wilf to Jason and Adam. 'Andy, Timmy, and I will just see what's left in the shop first,'

'Will it be safe for them,' asked Adam nervously. 'I don't' want to lose Andy when I've just found him?'

'If we think there will be a problem, we'll turn back I promise but, I've been that way a few times and sadly no one's there,' answered Wilf. 'Don't worry I'd never put the boys in danger.'

The next morning was a bit blustery, the trees bending in the wind, but Wilf Andy and Timmy set off early for the hours' drive. Sadly, they were used to empty small towns now. As they drew up by the music shop Andy noted there was a shop next door also abandoned, but with rolls of cloth that didn't look too damaged in the window, which were still intact. The scavengers hadn't found this town yet, and Andy knew cloth was scarce and took a long while to make by hand. So, he called to Wilf. 'Can we take some back I'm sure we'll have room.'

Wilf was in his element, and just nodded. There were several guitars, flutes, recorders, and keyboards, two sets of drums and a baby grand piano in the deserted shop. 'I wish we could take that,' he said to the boys, 'but it won't fit in my van.'

'There's a small lorry outside, if it starts, we could use that,' said Timmy.

'We can't do that,' said Wilf. 'How would we get our van home?'

'I've been driving tractors and Land Rovers since I was four.' said Timmy grinning and, 'Andy can drive too.'

'Maggie will not be happy if I let you drive,' said Wilf

knowing the tongue lashing he would get from Maggie if he let the boy's drive.

'She won't know till we get back, will she? and that lorry will take most of the music shop stock, then we can fill our van with cloth and wool. Come on let's see if the lorry goes, there must be key fobs inside,' said Timmy reasonably.

To their delight the lorry started and had a full charge as the electric had still been connected to most buildings. One of the plus points of the electric system being protected, and many places were already generating their own.

Timmy and Andy helped wheel out the piano and put it on the hoist to get it into the lorry. Then Andy started filling their own van with the contents of the other shop while Timmy helped Wilf. He found three sewing machines and decided to take the full drawers from the chests, as they were filled with useful items such as reels of cotton and pins, and loaded them too.

It took them two hours to empty the two shops but once the van and lorry were full Wilf backed out the lorry and with trepidation gave his van keys to Timmy. Luckily, they were both tall boys and the van was electric, so it was easy to drive. The drive was uneventful, much to Wilf's relief.

There was a group waiting for them when they got back, and Maggie showed admirable restraint, in not saying anything when the boys jumped down from the van. Although Wilf was a little concerned at what she would say when they were alone.

Andy ran to her took her hand and dragged her to the back of the van. 'Look at what I found,' he said, showing her what he had in the back. 'Do you think the dressmaker or tailor in the village would like some of this?'

Maggie looked on in amazement. 'Andy,' she said. 'How brilliant that you realised how useful all this would be. 'I could do with one of those sewing machines myself,' she smiled as Andy blushed at her praise. 'I can make a new dress now and the children's clothes as they grow. What a treat that will be.' She gave Andy a big hug and said to his dad who was helping unload, 'he's a credit to you, I'm so happy you are all staying. I don't know what I would have done if Andy left. The children have changed our lives from what was a bleak future, to one with hope.'

CHAPTER FORTY-EIGHT

It took Wilf a bit of time with Andy's Dad and brothers help, to get the studio up and running. Timmy had to go home but had messaged that they all wanted to go to a concert. It would be a good break after the months of work they had endured. Two of the adults could play the guitar, and another one a keyboard. Several wanted to join the choir, and some of the younger ones a band. Wilf suggested he bring some music over, and they could work out together what songs they needed to practice. This was giving everyone a much-needed boost.

At the village, Josh and Ginny were excited too after hearing about Wilfs concert. They wanted to sing, and Lewis could play the drums. Their music would wake the village up a bit, Ginny thought grinning to herself. This was going to be fun.

'What are you giggling to yourself about Ginny? Come on share, we're all ears.' Josh said, indicating the group of teenagers surrounding them.

'I think we should do a bit of our own music don't you?' Keep it a secret and add it at the last minute. That could be quite interesting,' said Ginny. 'We'd have to let Wilf in on it though, as we would need his studio and equipment to practice. Do you think he would keep quiet about it?'

'He'll be here soon we can ask him. If he doesn't agree we'll do it anyway, but it won't be quite as easy,' said Josh with a grin to the group surrounding him. 'Meet again after we've spoken to Wilf. '

~

'This is just what the village needs,' Val said to Jenny. 'A bit of music and some fun. Engaging with the Rick and Sues' farms and Wilf's community has been good for the village. I'm expecting Wilf soon.'

Wilf had been bringing fish to the farm for Edward to distribute for some time now, and was due soon, but this time was bringing Andy, Timmy, and some instruments.

'Do you think this concert should be here.' Jenny asked Val. 'How safe is it to have it at our farm? I'm a bit nervous after our talk to Sherebar and Joe. Here's Wilf now we'll have to tell him what Joe thinks,' said Val giving Wilf a wave.

'Hi Wilf, we were just talking about you,' said Jenny.

'Hope it was something good,' said Wilf with a smile, I just dropped the boys of with the other youngsters. They all seem to be quite excited from the noise I heard. I left some instruments with them, so it'll be interesting what they come up with.'

'When we heard about the concert we spoke to Joe about security as we were a bit concerned', said Val. 'He's come up with a compromise as I told Joe everyone needs a bit of fun. The last few months have been so hard. We've agreed to use the big Barn, not our field. Edwards okayed it, and we must extend our security barrier to cover it.' She said her voice solemn. 'Can you work with that?'

'Yes,' answered Wilf with conviction. 'We'll make it work; it's been so inspiring to see all the enthusiasm from the children. Are there any other survivors around that you know of who may want to join in?'

'We've looked in the local vicinity,' said Val. 'I'd thought we would find more, considering the number we vaccinated, but so far we haven't found any, maybe they moved away, been kidnapped by Thor, or hide when anyone comes near.'

She sighed, absentmindedly rubbing her stomach. 'I know the Government has people running the chicken and pig farms at Thetford, but we haven't been that way, they haven't been this way either. Too much to do here for the time being for us to venture far, but we must think about it soon. We can't live our lives in fear and isolation for ever, it's not healthy for the youngsters.' She looked at Jenny who nodded her agreement. 'Sherebar, or Joe may be able to tell us more, but to be fair, we haven't looked very hard. The Government must want all the farms possible to be working and productive. It must be a nightmare to feed the cities. I'm surprised we haven't seen more activity around,' continued Val.

'Do you know how others are coping? asked Wilf. 'We don't get any news where we are, and have been careful to keep a low profile so far. We didn't want to draw attention to ourselves either. It would be a bit difficult to cancel the concert now though, as everyone is so excited about it. I didn't realise I would get such a response. I hope it doesn't cause a problem. It would be good to know if there are others around managing too.'

'I don't know about the cities, but there is another area controlled by Thor according to Joe. I think that's the main priority of the Government. I'm not sure where it is, Sherebar's worried about it,' explained Jenny. 'Unless they can overcome them, we will always be fearful, and I for one can't live like that forever. 'Doug wants to open one of the abandoned Hospitals with his old partners who have been in touch, people don't stop being ill, even when they are immune to the virus. Doug thinks there's equipment lying around that he could still make use of. That may bring more people to the area if they have the skills to survive here. It would be interesting to have more neighbours.

They were interrupted by an exuberant Andy; he ran up to Wilf tugging at his sleeve. 'Come on Wilf,' he said,' we've got something to show you.'

Wilf looked at Jenny and Val, gave a good-natured shrug of his shoulders and followed Andy to meet the other teenagers.

Jenny and Val looked at each other and burst out laughing lightening the atmosphere. 'Teenagers,' said Jenni, 'They don't change.'

'Have you spoken any others about how safe this concert will be?' asked Jenny suddenly serious. 'There will be extra people here and we've been so careful so far.'

'It's a risk,' answered Val but let's go and talk to Edward and the engineers now and see if we can find a way to do this without too much aggravation.

CHAPTER FORTY-NINE

When Wilf arrived, the youngsters were all running around one of Edwards fields and Pegasus ambled over to see what was happening, seemingly not at all worried about the noise. Buster and Cassie were tearing around with Toby and David Joshua. The sun was shining and if those gathered hadn't been aware of the true situation, it would look as if life was back to the old normal. A group of the younger children were listening to the village music teacher and deciding what they should sing.

Beckoning to Wilf she said, 'do you have time to listen to this? They've chosen the song themselves.'

'Quiet!' shouted Wilf to those nearby. 'I want to listen to this.'

The words to 'somewhere over the rainbow', rose into the air, the young joyful voices carrying in the wind to those around who stopped to listen.

'That was beautiful,' said Wilf. What made you choose that? It's such an old song.'

'We'd been watching old movies on the village screens,' the teacher said, 'and the children liked it. I thought it was quite appropriate today and thought the adults would like it too.'

'Could you find another three to add to it?' queried Wilf. It would make a good younger section to the programme.'

'What do you think children, would you like to do that?' asked the teacher.

'Yes', they all shouted as they went off to play with David and the dogs.

The teenagers were arguing over who should play what instrument, so Wilf went over to audition them and find out if any of them had instruments of their own. A surprising number had something they could use and had formed small bands of their own.

'I want each group to find three songs, and I will be back in two weeks to hear what you have done. Any of you needing to use my studio are welcome, but it needs to be booked,' announced Wilf. 'The concert is in seven weeks if you are ready, eight, if you need more time. Remember this is supposed to be fun so don't argue about it.' With that Wilf left to talk to the adults who wanted to join in.

Eight weeks passed quickly, and everybody wanted to help. Hannah was going to make pancakes on her stall. There were going to be toffee apples and the bakery was providing cream teas with homemade scones and cream from Edwards's farm, a paddling pool with floating ducks and fishing rods, Edward and some of his workers had made a stage in the barn.

People started arriving and the excitement was building, the younger children opened the concert with three of their songs then it was the turn of the adults.

Wilf thought it was going very well, everyone seemed to be enjoying themselves, it was an outlet after all they'd been through. Then it was the turn of Josh and Ginny and their friends. Ginny In her usual colourful attire, bounded on the stage with a wave of exuberant music traveling around the barn. The audience danced everyone animated.

Then the music suddenly stopped, and Maggie went to the piano. Ella picked up a violin and Lewis a clarinet. The audience became silent wondering what was happening. With a nod from Wilf, Maggie started to play, Ella and Lewis joined in as David Joshua climbed on the stage taking Ginny's hand. Then Ginny began to sing. Her voice reaching up to the heavens in magical notes, Josh and David Joshua joining in. They had sung of regret and longing, of hope and love and a promised future. It was haunting and beautiful and full of emotion.

As it reached crescendo, tears were streaming unchecked down Ginny's face. David Joshua looked up at her and squeezed her hand. 'It's okay Ginny,' he whispered.

She looked down at him, squeezed his hand and pulled him close.

The audience erupted into applause as Hannah helped Ginny from the stage.

'How did you keep that a secret; it went straight to my heart,' said Hannah

That was the most amazing thing I have ever heard.'

'Wow,' exclaimed Edward, as he and Val joined the small group, with Jenny and Doug not far behind.

'Wilf and Maggie helped,' said Josh, 'but Ginny, Ella, David Joshua, and I wrote the song.'

'David Joshua!' queried, Val

'Yes,' grinned Josh. 'He sure has a way with words for a little boy.'

Wilf and Maggie joined them, and Jenny said, giving him a hug.

'Thank you so much. This was marvellous, something we all needed and will never forget.'

'We could start a joint choir and band if anyone's interested,' said Wilf 'Now we have reconnected with music it would be a shame to stop.'

'It would be good to get together to work this out,' agreed Doug, 'music played a big part in the wellbeing and doctors practice I had, before the virus destroyed so many lives.'

CHAPTER FIFTY

Miles away in Thor's headquarters a tall man with aquiline features was pacing up and down. Not having the compunction of his contemporary's such as Sherebar, to help those on earth. He, and a few others with his views, decided they liked this place but wanted to control it. The knowledge of the virus had been a bonus as the resulting chaos allowed Thor to expand. Up until now they had a few setbacks but nothing to cause much concern, until now. He was furious and not in any mood to accept excuses. The room was stark with a desk and two chairs, screens covered the walls, and pictures of the destroyed holding compound and Apis warehouse just added to his fury.

One of his Commanders stood before him quaking in his shoes. Those working for Thor had only just begun to realise the power, these strange people who controlled Thor possessed. He sometimes wondered what he and his fellow workers had got themselves into. He hoped the news he was bringing would help to temper the rage he felt coming his way in waves across the room. He could feel the perspiration caused by his fear running in rivulets down his back.

'Well, I hope you have something useful to say or you will soon be an ex-Commander, and I guarantee you won't like the place I am thinking of sending you,' said the man in charge in a voice full of malice.

'I've found the village where the group causing us so much problem come from. They are well protected and not visible, but they must feel safe because we picked up a trace of a gathering in a lowly protected area,' said the commander with more confidence than he felt.

'How do you know that's where they come from?' said the Boss in a calmer voice.

'Nowhere else in that area has that amount of camouflage, and we've had trouble with a couple of farms nearby,' argued the Commander. We've swept the area several times with our equipment, but it's always come back as largely uninhabited. The area wasn't showing much activity so was considered low priority. The cover they have is good, if we hadn't been taking another look, we wouldn't have found it.'

'Low priority by who?' Sneered the Boss. 'Call a meeting in one hour. I want a resolution to this problem now, sort out a plan. This problem's gone on too long.' With that he left the room.

The Commander heaved a sigh of relief as his boss left. He only had a hunch nothing concrete, that the anomaly was the hiding place of the group causing Thor trouble. He was under no illusion of his fate if he was wrong. Down one of the mines with the other unfortunates, would be the best he could expect.

CHAPTER FIFTY-ONE

In Sherebar's underground facility they were also discussing tactics, but in a more inclusive atmosphere.

The room was more comfortable than Thor's stark room. A large table in the middle, seating Sherebar, six of his compatriots, Joe, Sally, The General, and a surprise to Joe and Sally, two representatives of the current Government, Jack Reed, and Rachel Howard.

'I have asked Jack and Rachel to be here as they will have to deal with the aftermath of any action we take,' said Sherebar. 'Thor will be regrouping and heavily protecting their headquarters. We must take this out, as it's the last large stronghold of Thor in Britain. Thor won't surrender easily, but I also have information they are going to attack Val's village soon, try to destroy it, and move their main Thor operation including the captives, to Africa.'

'What do we do then?' asked Joe. 'We can't let them attack the village, can we?

'No', said The General joining in the conversation, 'but if we choose the same time to attack their headquarters, there will be less protection there. We need to destroy them once and for all, or they will be a thorn in our backside for the foreseeable future. We must finish them in Britain now. The village Shield is strong and should hold, we can monitor progress and redeploy if needed.'

'Okay,' said Joe who wasn't too happy with that. 'I'll go along with the suggestion, but need to make sure in my mind we have a good chance of success and be ready to help the village if necessary.' He looked at Sally who gave a slight nod in agreement.

'Our information is that we have six days to prepare as they're building up their forces, but I think we should go sooner, as I'm not sure Thor will wait that long,' said Sherebar. 'But remember all those in charge of Thor have the same abilities as me, and my friends here, indicating the others round the table. 'We'll need to protect our thoughts, and there is no doubt that Thor will do the same. I am going to contact their Controller and try to find out more. You can monitor the visit on our screens but remain silent.' With that Sherebar disappeared from the room.

The Controller of Thor was sitting at his desk when there was a movement in his room and Sherebar appeared.

'Decided to see how things should be done Sherebar?' said the man with a sneer. I'm surprised you got through our defences and risked a visit. I'll have to have a word with my security. Someone's been lax.'

'You can't hurt me Luka,' said Sherebar to the controller, 'so don't waste the effort of trying. Why are you doing this?' asked Sherebar in a reasonable voice. 'You are using some of the worst of humans, as enforcers. It was irresponsible to vaccinate them. You may not think it now, but you will regret it. The people of Britain that are left, will not just lie down, and give in to you. You could be fighting them for years despite your advanced mind. We have the whole universe at our fingertips, and I haven't given up my life so far, to see renegades of my race to undo the good we've done.'

'I like this planet,' replied Luka with conviction. 'You may have had some success at causing me problems so far, but you won't win the next one. We have units all over the planet. You won't be able to destroy them all. Leave now, you're irritating me we have nothing more to say to each other.'

With that he left the room.

With great sadness Sherebar's Hologram departed.

He had a lot to think about before he re-joined the others in the conference room. Standing in silence he drew in energy from his surroundings stilling his aura and relaxing his body.

Controlling his breathing he calmly opened the door and joined the others.

CHAPTER FIFTY-TWO

Those in the conference room looked up expectantly as Sherebar entered the room. Rachel and Jack were most concerned as to what would happen next. The General had kept them up to date in the seriousness of the next step against Thor. This was their first visit to Sherebar's facility, and they were a bit overwhelmed with some of the things they had seen. Partly, as they realised, the trouble the country would have been in if they hadn't had Sherebar on their side. They had their suspicions about The General too, Was he of Sherebar's race? Something Jack wasn't entirely sure of.

'As if we don't have enough to deal with,' Jack whispered to Rachel. He wasn't sure what the next step would be. He realised some of the people he had met had ability's not usual in the normal population, and he was lucky to have this group of them on his country's side. This facility was an amazing place, he had never seen anything like it. He and Rachel had been given a tour of the laboratories and workshops and realised how much these people had helped save many lives.

The General and Joe thought Thor would accelerate their attack on the village that Val and Jenny lived in, having found the location.

'This is the plan I've drawn up,' said The General as he pointed to the screen on the wall, that showed pictures of Thor's headquarters in particularly good detail. 'We have been successful in neutralising Thor so far, and if we succeed in destroying their headquarters. I'm sure they will rethink their position here. However, that doesn't mean that they won't increase their capability in the rest of the world, and we should be aware of that.' He paced the room, his strength of purpose coming through in his voice. 'If everyone's in agreement we need to begin preparations now and ready the Black Hawks. We need to go in three days' time.'

The Village was waiting for the attack they knew was coming, Joe had warned them to be ready. Thor had found the village, he said in his message. They blamed it as the instigator of al the troubles they'd had in Britain. Their headquarters had been attacked and although Sherebar's base was too powerful to destroy, they saw the village as an easy target. This was going to be their revenge before they moved to easier targets.

Mike the Engineer, and Ella's Dad, George, had joined Jenny, Doug, Val, Edward, and the others in the control room.

'They're coming and using their captives as a shield,' shouted Jenny, as she watched in horror the advance of Thor on the screens in the control room. The atmosphere was tense. They were prepared and The General and his men were on their way, as they had managed to disable Thor's headquarters, but would Freddie and his men be in time?

'Do you think our shield will hold? Jenny asked Mike

worriedly. 'What do we do about the captives? We can't just watch them die.'

Mike and George looked at each other both having the same idea. They had taken over the management of the shield, as it was not constantly used now. This was to enable the villagers to venture out more into the surrounding countryside. They couldn't slip in and out as Josh, Ginny, and the others with their special abilities could.

'It will take some precise timing and some of Thor's guards may get through so there needs to be a welcoming party for them, but I think it could work.' Said Mike as he explained his thoughts to the others.

They watched as the terrified Captives were urged forward.

Val, Jenny, Josh, Ginny, and David Joshua sent calming thoughts to the captives, telling them to run when told to.

As the captives were brutally pushed forward into to shield. Mike shouted, 'now.'

Val and the others sent forceful instructions to run, and the captives fell through the shield, as Mike shouted. 'Up.' and the shield was reinstated behind them.

There were many terrified people jumbled on the ground trying to stand up as the few guards that went through with them were rounded up and shackled.

There were villagers ready to help the captives away from the reinstated shield They were taken to the village hall where they were welcomed with food and drink. Not understanding what had just happened.

Some of the captives wanted to help when they realised they were saved. Some insisted there had to be something they could do. There was no way they were going to go back to what they had endured, but most were not in the physical condition to do so.

Thor gave a roar of frustration, their headquarters had

been attacked, their dream of controlling Britain crumbling. Those who thought it would be easy had been surprised by the resistance, not realising that there were more with extra resources than they realised.

'Dam Sherebar,' yelled the Controller. This was all his fault, he should have joined Thor, he had underestimated Sherebar's commitment to his decedents.

Thor readied to attack again, Hawks sweeping over the troops when two larger Black Hawks appeared above them. They didn't engage but white beams shot down locking the smaller Hawks in their beam, immobilising them and making them useless in the advance.

Then to the astonishment of Thor, and all those watching from the control room and village, music surrounded everyone. It wasn't the same as that used to bring the buildings down in the Thor compound. Unbeknown to those present this was being relayed throughout the world.

The world stopped and listened. It was the most beautiful sound that was impossible to describe. Everyone on both sides (Thor and the Village) stood still in amazement.

Waves of calm was felt by all.

Then a voice full of sadness and sorrow, that was inexplicably understood by everyone, resonated around the world.

'You were not sent here to fight, you were here to help bring in a new age,' said the voice to Thor in all its locations. 'You have access to the Universe and all its wonders, and have forgotten, in your haste to dominate, your purpose here.'

'To the people of the World, there will be no more war, your missiles will not work. You have been given a second chance, use it wisely. You have a choice to take it or not, but be under no illusion, if you disregard this warning humanity will disappear from this earth. '

'As a race you have a brain of which you use a fraction. Gradually unlocking this is the task of mankind. You have misused my bounty and will be limited in production of your species. The children born in the future will be the legacy of this time. They will be few, and all should take care of them. Called the Indigo generation they are the future of the world.

With that the voice disappeared and Thor's army looked round in amazement as their commanders disappeared and small white orbs rose into the air as the smaller hawks drifted to the ground.

No longer in the thrall of superior minds, the men left surrendered to the Generals army who had just arrived.

W*ell, that was interesting* the General thought, *what now for the armies of the world.* He looked around at the chaos surrounding him and gave orders to his men to round up the survivors. 'I've some transport arriving to take them where they can be questioned,' he said to one of his officers with a grimace. Not something he was looking forward to. He looked up as Joe approached. 'What did you make of that Joe? The General questioned.

'You know better than me, don't you?' answered Joe taking a huge breath and shaking himself to get rid of the stress he was still feeling. 'You're one of Sherebar's race, aren't you?'

The General just smiled, patted Joe on the back and walked off to join his men.

Joe stared after him, shrugged his shoulders and went to find his sisters Val and Jenny.

EPILOGUE

The villagers were ecstatic, and an impromptu party began. The Thor captives were found clothes, although it was quite a mismatch as there were so many, nobody seemed to mind, as a carnival atmosphere prevailed. Someone found the BBQ's and dug out sausages from the store, a guitar was playing, and drums could be heard in the background.

Val, Jenny, Doug, and Edward were in the control room. All were relieved at the outcome of the conflict with Thor but were wary of getting too excited.

Where did the voice come from, could they believe what was said and who were the Indigo Children?

At that moment Josh and Ginny burst through the door coming to a stop when they saw the expression on the groups face.

'What's the matter,' asked Josh.

'Did I hear you mention the Indigo children?' said Ginny.

'What do you know about them?' enquired Val with trepidation.

'Well,' they said together looking at each other wondering

what to say, 'it's a bit of a story, something you need to talk to Sherebar about.'

Just Then Val felt a kick in her stomach as if Star was saying don't forget about me. Was she an Indigo child Val wondered? A question she would perhaps find an answer to in the coming years. Where Ginny and Josh indigo children too. They were special, what was their future? She couldn't see them happy to stay in the village for ever. She loved them but they had their own life to lead.

The group looked at each other, for now, they agreed they would live with the new reality. it couldn't be worse than the past. Could it?

SHEREBAR

BOOK 1

CHAPTER 1

The room was dark and musty; the only light came from the moon shining through the large French doors and the glow of the dying embers of the fire. The high ceilings were yellowed with age, the walls dark with the smoke of countless candles burnt in days gone by. It was cold, but not cold enough for the young girl curled up on the battered leather armchair to move.

She was mesmerised by the portrait of an old gentleman that was hanging over the fireplace. His costume was from an era she didn't recognise, a long blue velvet cloak with silver buckles covering most of his angular frame, his abundant grey hair curling gently on his collar. He was holding his hat in one hand and a flat silver-coloured disc in the other, which didn't seem at all odd to her at that time, a dog at his feet, but it was the eyes she couldn't turn away from. They seemed to devour her, following every move she made, making her feel shivery and uneasy. She thought how stupid that was, it was only an old painting after all, and told herself to move, but somehow, she couldn't. His presence seemed to fill the room, pulling her to him through space and time. His name was Sherebar.

Jenny woke up with the usual sense of foreboding she always had with this recurring dream. For a moment she couldn't remember where she was. The duvet was crumpled where she had tossed and turned, her short dark curls plastered to her head with perspiration, her body aching as if she had been in a violent confrontation. I must try and remember all the details, she thought. Perhaps that way she could dispel the fears that seemed to haunt her sleep. That was easier said than done she realised.

She recalled dreaming of a young girl with whom she felt a kinship but didn't know why. There was a portrait she was certain had an important message for her, if only she could understand it. It was very perplexing and frightening.

Then there was a dramatic change of scene, a feeling of falling slowly through a dark, misty tunnel, difficulty breathing, claustrophobia and a smell she couldn't identify.

Suddenly, she had found herself in a large cavern lit by a shaft of sunlight streaming through a crack in the rocky roof. There was tension in the air and her stomach had contracted with fear and foreboding. She had to fight hard to control the sickness welling up to engulf her.

This time she hadn't been chased by the unnamed foes that tried to grab her hair and pull at her clothes that haunted her usual nightmares. As her eyes had grown accustomed to the dim light, she had been surprised to see three figures standing around a large pool of water.

'Come,' beckoned one of the three, a slight girl with blonde hair, wearing a red dress that shone like delicate gossamer. 'We've been waiting for you; now we can begin.'

Jenny had walked slowly towards them, wondering who they were, they seemed familiar; it was as if she knew them, but frustratingly couldn't remember their names. Looking down, she'd been unsurprised to find that, like the other girls, she was clad in a kaftan style dress, but hers was vibrant shimmering blue. The material was soft and clung to her as she moved.

'What do I do?' she had asked, shivering with anxiety, sensing the tension in the air. 'Why am I here? Who are you?'

'Don't be afraid, you are needed here; hold our hands,' said the other blonde girl, dressed in yellow, who seemed to dance in the glow of sunbeams.

Jenny trembled and felt another shaft of fear as the air stilled. Biting cold enveloped her as a howl echoed through a crack in the cavern's rocky walls, the only other sounds the drip, drip of the stalactites into the pool, and the ominous flapping of disturbed bats.

In an instant, the shaft of light disappeared as if a switch had been turned off and plunged the cavern in darkness. It was still, so still; nothing moved, and Jenny was paralysed with terror. Slowly a chill crept up her spine, making the hair on her neck stand on end. 'He's near, he's coming for me, help me,' she screamed, as ice cold fingers probed her body and something sinister and dangerous tried to take control of her mind. She was choking, gasping to breathe, as invisible hands closed around her throat as she started to lose consciousness, the dark figure of her dreams was there as she feared.

'Together we are the elements, air, water, fire, and earth. This is our strength; we call on the universe to come to our aid,' cried the girl in the red dress. Her voice was strong and true as it resonated around the cave and seemed to have a powerful strength of its own.

The cave pulsed with the power being unleashed. A waterspout rose from the pool and took on the form of a giant man glowing in the dark, teeth like fangs and hollow eyes full of death.

'Hold our hands and feel the power. We are the four and that is our protection,' chanted the three girls.

The third girl, brown-haired and dressed in green, the colour of a forest in spring, said forcefully, 'He can't hurt you, Jenny; shut him out, push out your fear. Focus on the power we are sending you.'

Jenny struggled to remain conscious and concentrate on the power flowing through the hands she held. The water-spout changed into a malevolent fog that was trying to envelop her as she tried to shake herself free, sending shock waves throughout her body that touched her soul. A black curtain of despair was gradually overtaking her, dulling her mind, and filling her with dread. Suddenly, she felt a surge of forceful energy, pushing out the darkness, and it was gone.

Jenny shook from cold and relief, and it was only the hands she held keeping her upright. The hands tightened on hers, giving her strength, and the light gradually increased to a golden glow. 'Be brave,' the girls said in unison. 'We need your sight, come dance with us and let your mind run free.'

All Jenny wanted to do after that experience was collapse on the floor and sleep, but they pulled her with them, and slowly they began to dance the sacred dance of gods of the past. Faster and faster, they whirled, colours twisting and turning, generating an energy that sent sparks flying in the still air.

Jenny felt an exhilaration she had never experienced before. She didn't know how she knew to dance like that, but it was instinctive and as the dance ended, they had sunk to the ground exhausted.

The brown-haired girl took Jenny's hand and, pulling her up, led her gently to a natural hollow in the rock that was full of sparkling water. As she gazed at it, it became silver like a mirror and still as death. 'Look into the mirror and tell us what you see. You are our channel to the future and the connection to our past.'

How is that? Jenny wondered, this is seriously weird, but instinctively knew she had to try.

At first, Jenny couldn't see anything, and then images began to appear, although it was difficult to make them out clearly. A swirling mist that gradually dissipated. A desolate countryside, derelict houses, everything dead except children, hungry and emaciated, crying for their parents. Jenny felt a terrible dread and unimaginable sadness. Was she seeing the future or the past?

This faded. Then she said, 'Rats in cages, they're ill and hurting. We must save them; they're trying to tell me something and they're frightened but want to help. I'm running, they're letting the rats out and want to kill them. I can't let that happen. Thousands of people will die.'

'Is it the plague?' asked the girl in red.

'No, it's worse, it's the end of everything I care about. I'm sorry, it's gone,' apologised Jenny as she slumped to the ground, all energy drained from her.

At this point, Jenny had woken up. She was sure that the girls in the dream were known to her, but who were they, where did they come from? Struggling to decipher the meaning, Jenny looked at the clock and realised that if she didn't get a move on, she would be late for work, and she had a client at nine o'clock.

CHAPTER 2

After showering quickly and pulling on grey trousers and a soft blue top, Jenny was about to put on her shoes when she noticed a small silver disc on her dressing table. Frowning, she picked it up. How did that get there? she wondered. Unless I'm going mad; it wasn't there last night. She checked her windows, locked as they should be no one could have come up the stairs without passing by Buster, her dog and security guard. He would have let her know if anyone had been in the house.

Damn, she thought. I haven't time to worry about this now. She put the disc in her pocket, put on her shoes, picked up her coat and ran down the stairs. Buster stood at the bottom, wagging his tail. 'We're late,' Jenny said as she rushed into the small kitchen, picking up a few cans of dog food as she went. Opening the door, she ushered Buster out before setting the alarm. They went through the side gate, making sure this was locked too, and into the car on the driveway.

Buster, a large cream German Shepherd, sat up in the back and proceeded to lick Jenny's ear by way of hello. 'Stop that. I want a word with you when we get to work. I want to know how that disc appeared in my room without you hearing anything,' scolded Jenny. Just thinking about it made the hair on her neck tingle. It wasn't a good feeling.

Work was a small office in a business centre on a trading estate, one of the new stylish ones, all metal and glass. They had been desperate for tenants as the recession had hit them hard, hence the allowance of Buster. He was too big to be left in Jenny's small house on his own, and ever since Jenny had worked for herself, he had come with her. Buster loved travelling in the car, and he seemed to understand every word Jenny said, especially 'dinner's ready'. It was almost as if there was telepathy between them.

The office was spacious, with two desks, one for the Mac used for designing and one for the PCs for general programming. The office had plenty of storage and lots of light. Jenny was a programmer and designer, and business was picking up. She was getting paid, at long last.

She gave Buster his breakfast and a big hug, got herself a coffee from the machine, which wasn't bad compared to some office coffee she'd tasted, sat at her desk, and switched on her computer. Jenny took a big gulp of coffee hoping it would give her a boost after the night she'd had. It feels cold in here today, I hope it warms up, she thought.

'Fifteen minutes before our first client, Buzzy,' she said. 'Just time for a quick browse.' Then Jenny froze, looking at her screen in horror. Buster gave a low growl. Running across on-screen was a large black rat. It stopped as if looking at her, its eyes dark and brooding, then disappeared. Jenny ran out to reception.

'Has anyone been in my office since I left?' she asked. 'Someone's been tampering with my computer.'

'That's impossible,' said Paul, the office building owner, who was currently manning the desk, as he liked to know all his tenants. 'You each have security keys and you know how tight security is here because of all the equipment around. I thought you had your own extra safeguards as well, because of the work you do?'

'I do,' said Jenny thoughtfully. 'Were the security cameras' in the corridors working last night?'

'Yes,' said Paul, 'and they don't look as if they have been tampered with. I'm sure you won't find anything, but do you want me to look for you anyway? I know I don't know as much about computers as you do, but can't things be sent from computer to computer?'

'Yes, but my problem can't. I'm careful about what I download; I have virus protection as well as my own security designed by Joe, my brother, but thanks anyway. Let me know if you find anything,' she said as she went back into her office.

Buster raised his head and came to sit by her as if knowing Jenny needed comfort. What's happening to me? Jenny thought. Am I hallucinating? Why am I so frightened? She put her hand in her pocket and felt the small disc. Well, this is real. What do I do with it? At that moment, there was a knock on the door and a man of about thirty-five, tall, blonde hair, well-built, with an open friendly face and an air of authority, entered.

'Hi, I'm Doug Francis,' he said, holding out his hand. 'Thanks for seeing me at short notice. It's the only time I have free. We had a real problem the other day and a new system for the surgery is rather overdue.'

Just as Jenny was about to take his hand, Buster got up and stood between them. Doug lowered his hand for Buster to sniff and laughed as Buster proceeded to lick him. 'Sorry about that; not terribly hygienic,' said Jenny with a smile. 'I hope you don't mind dogs. He's very protective and likes to vet my clients.'

'No, I like dogs and wish I could have one myself, but he

won't be able to come to the surgery if you need to go there; will that be a problem?' Doug asked.

'He stays here with Paul or Molly on Reception if I'm out, so that's okay. Would you like a coffee and then perhaps we should start? I need to get as much

CHAPTER 3

Jenny and Doug worked all morning and, apart from a few phone calls, there were no interruptions. The system required was quite complex, but Jenny had recently devised a similar one that was being used in some other businesses. It just needed adaptation and would save the practice time once the information had been entered. It would ensure there would always be a record of drugs supplied and patient history, flagging up any conflicts. It would also highlight if there were any pockets of illness, enabling doctors to vaccinate or target patients in certain areas before it became too widespread, thus saving time and money.

Being proactive rather than reactive was something Jenny realised Doug was passionate about, as he explained his thinking to her. Preventive medicine may not be the current buzzword but if he could make sure his practice acted at the right time, it would translate into less hospital beds being required. It made sense to Jenny, and she was sure it was something she could help him with.

When Jenny felt Doug had supplied as much information

as he could to be going on with, she suggested a break for lunch. She left Buster sleeping and took Doug to a café around the corner. It was bright, not too expensive and the food was all home cooked. Over large plates of steaming, creamy pasta and crisp green salad drizzled with aromatic olive oil and balsamic vinegar, Jenny, who was normally a very private person, found herself telling Doug all about her recurring dreams and the fear that came with them. He was easy to talk to. He drew information out of her in a way that only her brother and sister could do.

'It's getting weird, and I'm exhausted from lack of sleep. Am I going mad?' she asked.

Doug smiled. 'Don't worry,' he said. 'It's probably just overwork combined with something you've seen or read.'

Jenny bit her lip. Should she tell him about the disc and the computer? Not yet, she thought. I don't know him well enough.

After lunch, they worked on until four o'clock and agreed to meet at the surgery in a week's time to check on progress. Jenny watched him go, thinking dreamily that he was the nicest man she had met in a long while. There had been no one special in her life for months. Buster had taken a distinct dislike to her last boyfriend, and she'd learnt to trust his judgement. Getting her business off the ground had taken a lot of time, work, and money, and not all men were understanding about late nights spent working, and broken dates.

Doug was interesting. Jenny liked his commitment to his staff and patients and the new ideas he was keen to introduce. Trying to integrate natural healing into his practice was brave, she thought. Doug and Val, her sister, would get on like a storm. Val, who was already using natural methods of healing in her veterinary practice, was getting great results. 'Stop daydreaming,' she told herself sternly, realising she still had a lot of work to do.

Towards the end of the day, Jenny sat at the computer, trying to gather her thoughts. She shut the computer down and then opened it again, but nothing happened. She looked through her systems. All seemed as it should be her checks were in place; and none of her passwords had been breached as far as she could tell. She let out a sigh, there was a ball of apprehension in the pit of her stomach. What should she do about the disc? She picked it up and it seemed to pulsate in her hand. She dropped it as if it was hot, reached a trembling hand towards the phone and rang her brother.

He answered on the second ring. 'Hi, Sis,' he said. 'What's up?'

'How do you know anything's up?'

'You don't usually ring this time of day unless there's a problem, and that's getting less and less. I've taught you well,' Joe said.

'I've got a problem, a big one, I need to see you soon. Can I come over tonight?' asked Jenny, trying to hide the fear she felt from showing in her voice.

'You're in luck. Sally's away for a few days and I'm starving. Throw in some food and I'm all yours. Bring that big brute of a dog too if you like; I've missed him since you moved out,' laughed Joe.

'Okay, I'll see you at about seven.' Jenny smiled at the thought of Joe coping on his own. Sally, his girlfriend, had been good for him. She understood his driving need to succeed and managed to balance this with common sense. He was a loner by inclination, clever with new technology, but also likeable and sociable in the right circumstances. He had strong views that he wasn't afraid to air, which had occasionally caused a few problems for him in the past.

Jenny had liked Sally the minute she had met her, and she was now very much part of their small family. Joe, Jenny, and Val had lived together after their parents and Uncle Jack had died in a car crash. Unbelievably, nobody had paid the price for their parents' deaths as the hit and run driver had never been caught. Their car had been pulled from the river, and the damage to the front of the car suggested a collision with something large and heavy. The siblings had been devastated, but they had clung to each other and somehow survived their grief, although the pain would always be there, surfacing every now and again to remind them of what they had lost.

Val had been the first to move out, as she needed to be nearer the veterinary practice she had bought and was developing. Then Joe had met Sally, and Jenny had felt it time to stand on her own feet. It had been hard, she had been lonely, but she was getting there. The three of them carried a strong sense of each other, as they had since they were born, and the bond between them was extremely strong. It had helped immensely in dealing with the tragedy of their parents' death. They were not in each other's pockets but would always help each other out if needed. Life had moved on but was quite different from the carefree one they had led before.

Jenny had another hour before she needed to leave but couldn't settle to work. Thoughts of her parents always unsettled her. She picked up her copy of the paper that reception delivered and idly flicked through it. An article caught her eye, and a shiver went through her. It was about the use of rats in experiments to find a gene that causes cancer. The picture of the black rat accompanying it seemed to stare right at her. She hated experiments on animals but accepted that she didn't know how she would feel if it was her mother, father or child that needed a breakthrough medicine. She thought of Val, who loved animals with a passion. No way would she ever use animals in her laboratory.

There must be another way, thought Jenny. It's stupid,

why am I so jumpy? She put the paper in the bin and called Buster. 'Let's go,' she said as she locked up. 'Enough for today. I think it's a large pizza and a bottle of wine. How does that sound to you?' Buster wagged his tail as any food was alright by him.

ALSO FROM M M JUNIPER

Also, from author, M M Juniper

The Sherebar series.

Book 1
Sherebar

Book 2
Sherebar. Betrayal of the innocent.

ABOUT THE AUTHOR

ABOUT THE AUTHOR

MM Juniper has been writing for most of her life. She lives by the coast with her husband and children and has two very energetic dogs! Her first adult fiction book Sherebar is the beginning of a three-part trilogy.

'A magical read! Full of mystery and drama. 5 stars!'

'I really enjoyed this book. I usually read romances, but do like to try new genres when recommended to them. This book is full of action to make you want to keep turning page after page.'

'A real mystery and such an intriguing story. Grab a copy! A great addition to any bookshelf and my mother in law has already asked to borrow my copy, so I will probably end up buying another one.'

Printed in Great Britain
by Amazon

26051675R00159